D0994712

AA

MINI GUIDE

Peak District

2ND EDITION

THE PENNINE WAY

Authors: Mike Gerrard
Verifier: Neil Coates

Project Management: James Harrison and Amanda Lunn
Proofreader and Indexer: Jo Weeks

For AA Publishing:
Managing Editor: David Popey
Picture Research: Liz Allen
Internal Repro and Colour Manipulation: Neil Smith
Production: Rachel Davis
Cartography provided by the Mapping Services Department of AA Publishing

Produced by AA Publishing
© AA Media Limited 2007
Reprinted 2008 and 2009
Updated and revised 2010

Published by AA Publishing (a trading name of AA Media Limited, whose registered office is Fanum House, Basing View, Basingstoke, Hampshire RG21 4EA; registered number 06112600)

 This product includes mapping data licensed from the Ordnance Survey® with the permission of the Controller of Her Majesty's Stationery Office. © Crown Copyright 2011. All rights reserved. Licence number 100021153.

A04587   ISBNs: 978-0-7495-6886-3 and 978-0-7495-6896-2 (SS)

A CIP catalogue record for this book is available from the British Library.

The contents of this book are believed correct at the time of printing. Nevertheless, the publishers cannot be held responsible for any errors or omissions or for changes in the details given in this book or for the consequences of any reliance on the information it provides. We have tried to ensure accuracy in this book, but things do change and we would be grateful if readers would advise us of any inaccuracies they may encounter. This does not affect your statutory rights.

Visit AA Publishing at theAA.com/shop

Printed in China by Everbest.

KINDER PLATEAU

CURBAR EDGE

CONTENTS

INTRODUCTION

Officially known as the Peak District, this extraordinary landscape has also been called The Hollow Country. It is an area riven by gorges and riddled by caverns; it is where lowland England erupts into upland splendour, haltered by endless miles and countless acres of bronze and purple-burnished moors, cliffs and scarps arcing to the horizon to meet with England's backbone, the lofty Pennines. The heart of England's first National Park is the White Peak, reflecting the pale-grey hues of the limestone bedrock. Beyond the gaping maw of Dovedale are undulating plateaux dotted by prehistoric monuments and threaded by field walls; here ash woods cascade into spectacular valleys where seasonal rivers flow with crystal-clear water in winter and green veins of butterbur during summer.

DOVEDALE

PUBLIC
FOOTPATH ONLY
MILLDALE
& DOVEDALE

INTRODUCTION

Beneath villages of silvery cottages set in abundant wildflower meadows, miners toiled for centuries, turning the landscape inside-out, discovering cave systems and unwittingly creating fascinating heritage locations that melt seamlessly into the backcloth.

Around the north, east and west of this timeless core sweep stunning escarpments and ridges of millstone grit, a rugged geological formation giving us the name of the Dark Peak. Vast moors dappled by reservoirs end in precipitous edges, over which waterfalls tumble into wooded vales that once echoed to the thrumming of industry.

The Peak District was the location for the world's first great textile mills, England's own silk industry and countless other enterprises that make this region a peerless area for industrial archaeology. Tucked below the scalloped edges of these moors are charming small towns and villages of three-storey weaver's cottages and soot-darkened church towers, where narrowboat trips offer ease of exploration whilst paths snake up to boundless moors haunted by white hares and the chuckling of grouse.

Traversing this former tribal domain – the word Peak comes from the Dark Ages Anglo-Saxon clan, the pecsaetan – are Britain's first and latest National Trails, the Pennine Way and Pennine Bridleway. The latter was Britain's first purpose-built, long-distance bridleway for riders, mountain bikers and walkers. Myriad other trails and walks combine with cycling routes, many based on former packhorse trails and railways, drawing together past and present.

Scratch the surface and the land that charmed and terrified authors and commentators from Daniel Defoe to George Eliot, Sir Arthur Conan Doyle to D H Lawrence is still there for the finding. The Hollow Country and its darker twin can enlighten and excite, educate and exhilarate.

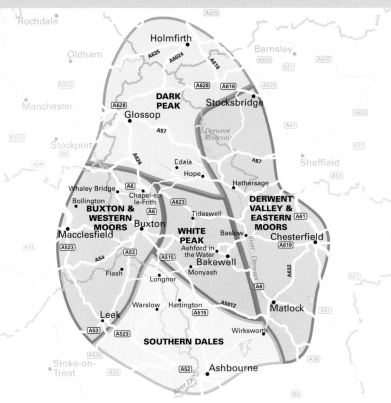

LADYBOWER RESERVOIR

ESSENTIAL SIGHTS

UNMISSABLE ATTRACTIONS

The Peak District, covering 555sq miles (1,438sq km), was designated as England's first National Park in 1951, reflecting its importance as a landscape of rare drama and beauty. Lead mining has left a legacy of discarded millstones and farming has shaped the open moors and created drystone-wall pastures. No other region of England has such diversity, busy with visitors and walkers yet full of wide open spaces where walkers, although close to large towns and cities, can feel as though they are at one with the wilderness.

1

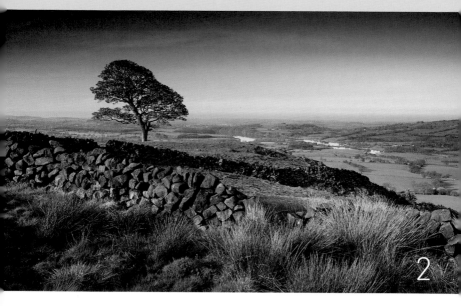

1 **Kinder Scout**
A hiker scrambles over gritstone slabs high above Kinder Reservoir at the western fringe of the Dark Peak. Nearby Hayfield is a steep climb to the moody plateau of Kinder Scout, the highest point in the National Park.

2 **Leek**
Enjoy far-reaching views, which take in green fields divided by drystone walls while gentle slopes lead down to the valley bottom in the countryside near the Roaches.

15

3

4 The River Dove Stepping Stones
Here, at the southern end of Dovedale, just east of the village of Ilam, are the stepping stones that cross the River Dove. This beauty spot is hugely popular with families who like to picnic near the river bank.

5 Ashbourne
Lively markets are a feature of many of the towns in the Peak District. In Ashbourne traders set up their stalls in Market Place on Thursday and Saturday.

3 Dovedale
This is one of the most beautiful and popular of all the limestone dales, with paths that range over windswept grassland hills to the deep shadows of the valley.

Day One in the Peak District

For many people a weekend break or a long weekend is a popular way to spend their leisure time. These eight pages offer a loosely planned itinerary designed to ensure that you make the most of your time and see and enjoy the very best the area has to offer.

Friday Night

If you can afford it, stay at Fischer's Baslow Hall hotel, just north of Baslow village on the A623, perched above the River Derwent. The food is superb: herbs freshly picked from the kitchen garden and succulent local venison, pork, beef and pigeon. In the evening you can go for a short drive and stroll on to Curbar Edge, for a view of the setting sun over the White Peak.

Saturday Morning

Along the A619 is the impressive entrance to Chatsworth Park. Spend the morning walking around the magnificent house and grounds, or explore East Moor and Beeley Moor. Here, you will fine excellent heather moorland, with Bronze Age settlements and barrows.

Return to Baslow and rejoin the A623, driving northwest up Middleton Dale, past Lovers' Leap and Baslow's tiny octagonal toll house.

LADYBOWER RESERVOIR

TIDESWELL

Saturday Lunch
Stop at the Three Stags' Heads pub at Wardlow Mires. This stone-floored pub serves well-kept beers from excellent independent Sheffield breweries. You'll find good food too, served on plates and dishes from the adjacent pottery.

Saturday Afternoon
Head for Tideswell, either by driving further along the A623 and turning off left, or by a side-road through the pretty village of Litton. Walk round the fine parish church at Tideswell ('Cathedral of the Peak') then take the car down to the Tideswell Dale car park and walk along Miller's Dale as far as Water-cum-Jolly Dale, with ash trees, limestone crags and the tinkling waters of the Wye.

Drive southwest on the B6049 and A5270 to meet the A515 and then go southeast to Parsley Hay. Turn left on minor roads for Youlgreave for a look at the great stone circle of Arbor Low – a ditch, bank and circle of 47 stones, now lying flat – and the nearby barrow of Gib Hill; both date from the Bronze Age. Return to the A515 and turn left; then right onto the B5054 to Hartington.

Saturday Night
Stay at Biggin Hall, located just one mile (1.6km) to the southeast of Hartington; it comprises a cluster of 17th-century buildings with mullioned windows and oak beams. If possible, try to book the Master Suite, complete with four-poster bed. In the morning, enjoy a traditional farmhouse breakfast using good locally produced ingredients.

21

Day Two in the Peak District

You are now in the heart of the White Peak, close to the southern dales. Your second day explores this beautiful area before heading north for a tour of the Dark Peak, with alternative options depending on your personal preferences and the weather.

Sunday Morning

Go for an early walk down Biggin Dale, or linger over breakfast and then look round Hartington; feed the ducks on the pond and buy some local cheese to take home. Then follow in the footsteps of the 'Compleat Anglers', Izaak Walton and Charles Cotton, down Beresford Dale on the quiet upper reaches of the River Dove. You can walk as far as you wish, into Wolfscote Dale and to Mill Dale, but for this you will need a packed lunch.

Further south still is famous Dovedale. If you wish you can drive to Ilam and take the easy short walk by the Stepping Stones to Mill Dale. But remember, this route is likely to be popular on a fine Sunday morning.

Sunday Lunch

From Hartington or Ilam head for Warslow (on the B5053), where you can call in for lunch at the Greyhound Inn, a traditional coaching inn popular for its home-cooked dishes. Warslow is close to the Manifold Valley; a short detour down minor roads into Ecton will give you a flavour of the scenery, and there is a visitor centre at the nearby old station at Hulme End.

Sunday Afternoon

Leaving Warslow, drive north on the A5053 to and through Longnor to reach the A515; here turn left to Buxton. There are now several options. If the weather is really unkind you can spend the afternoon here, breezing around the Pavilion Gardens or visiting Poole's Cavern. Return to Baslow via the A6 south, Bakewell and then the A619.

Alternatively, head north on the A6 through Dove Holes, turn right onto the A623 and then fork left at The Wanted Inn to reach Castleton via the dramatic Winnats Pass road. In Castleton, there are caves and Blue John mines, the oldest castle in the Peak and good pubs and cafés.

Or, if you are feeling adventurous and there is no risk of blizzards stay on the A6 north to Chapel-en-le-Frith then north on the A624 to Glossop. Turn east on the A57, crossing the Snake Pass and dropping down the Woodlands Valley to the Derwent Dams. Whichever way you go, finish at Padley Gorge (Grindleford) close to where you started, in the shade of sessile oaks and with pied flycatchers singing among the branches.

TISSINGTON

Southern Dales

ASHBOURNE

CARSINGTON WATER

DOVEDALE

HARTINGTON

ILAM

LONGNOR

MANIFOLD VALLEY

TISSINGTON

WIRKSWORTH

INTRODUCTION

The arc of countryside from Leek through Ashbourne to Belper rolls and dips southwards to the Trent river plain, while its tributary the Dove meanders through fields and hedgerows. On the far side of Ashbourne, however, everything changes as the land rises and the Dove spreads out a thousand fingers into every crevice of the hills. Brooks and rivulets reach into the limestone at the Peak's core. Villages lie on the thousand-foot contour on the plateau because the valleys are so narrow; ancient ash woods clothe the slopes, cattle graze the pastures and drystone walls cobweb the meadows.

28

DOVEDALE

ESSENTIAL SIGHTS

Unmissable attractions

Ashbourne, a market town, celebrated for its gingerbread, is at the gateway to Dovedale, the most famous and popular of all the dales. This 7-mile (11.3km) stretch, from the Stepping Stones to Hartington is best avoided at peak holiday times but the quieter upper reaches can be explored from the little hilltop village of Longnor, which sits atop a ridge between the Dove and Manifold. There are many good walks from this charming village, including the reef limestone hills of Chrome and High Wheeldon to the east. Just to the south is the twisting gorge of the Manifold Valley, which has one of several cycle rides that follow the tracks of disused railways.

1

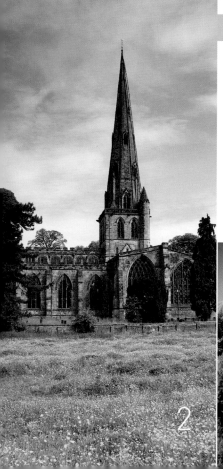

1 **Dovedale**
A path follows the River Dove as it winds its quiet way below the limestone peaks.

2 **Ashbourne**
St Oswald's Church in Ashbourne with its tall spire (212 feet/65m), is one of Derbyshire's grandest.

3 **Manifold Valley**
Spectacular Thor's Cave dominates the centre of the Manifold Valley.

Millennium Clock

THE ASHBOURNE GINGERBREAD SHOP

Natural Choice

ASHBOURNE

ASHBOURNE

The old market town of Ashbourne is located in a cleft in the rolling farmland of southwest Derbyshire. it lies in a landscape of fields and hedges rather than moors and walls. Along this green cleft runs the Henmore Brook on its way to meet the River Dove.

The drive into and through Ashbourne is not straightforward; there is a one-way system and the roads are often congested, but there are points on the sweeping drive down into the town where the shape of the settlement can be appreciated. The most immediate impression is that the parish church, with its distinctive needle-sharp spire, is some way from the town centre. This means that when you have parked your car, there is a walk of several hundred yards if you want to take a close look at the famous St Oswald's, but by doing so, and exploring the Market Place on the way, you see the very best that this town has to offer.

Visit

'OAKBOURNE'

Ashbourne is a perfect example of an English market town – eccentric street plan, narrow cobbled alleys, coaching inns, almshouses and market stalls. It needed very little alteration to become George Eliot's Oakbourne in *Adam Bede*, and is probably the best place in the Peak District to explore for antiques.

Ashbourne Market Place, opposite the Town Hall, used to be lined with alehouses and, at one time, had its own bullring (close to the Wright Memorial, an elaborate piece of Victoriana). It was here that Bonnie Prince Charlie proclaimed his father King of England, and it was from here that the famous Shrovetide Football, between the 'Uppards' and 'Downards' of the town, always started. It was moved to Shaw Croft to reduce damage to property, but still rages along the Henmore, between the goals of

Sturton Mill and Clifton Mill, each Easter. At the back of the Market Place is the Old Vaults pub, which used to be called The Anatomical Horse, with a skeleton for its sign. Down the narrow alley to the left is Victoria Square (once The Butchery and The Shambles) and Tiger Yard, beside a restaurant that used to be The Tiger Inn. The modern Victoria Square is a smart little suntrap, set about with benches.

Ashbourne's side streets and alleys are narrow and interesting; the layout of the old town north of the Henmore dates back to the 11th and 12th centuries and there are some fascinating nooks and crannies to explore, such as Lovatt's Yard and the House of Confinement (a lock-up) on Bellevue Street. However, it is along St John's Street and Church Street that the town's grandest buildings are to be found. Beyond the Clergy's Widows Almshouses are superb mansions and merchants' houses, several now serving as antiques shops,

culminating in the magnificent stone-gabled Grammar School, founded by Elizabeth I in 1585. And opposite, set behind tall wrought-iron gates and a carpet of daffodils in the spring, stands St Oswald's. It was built around 1340 and perfectly described by the novelist George Eliot as 'the finest mere parish church in England'.

CARSINGTON WATER

New reservoirs usually take years to blend with a landscape, and sometimes they never do. Carsington, opened by Her Majesty the Queen in 1992, already looks at home in the gently rolling hills southwest of Wirksworth.

Most of the Peak District's many reservoirs gather their water from acid moorland, so they are low in nutrients, and this in turn means they are poor for aquatic plants and animals. However, Carsington is quite different: it is filled largely by water pumped from rivers and so is excellent for wildlife. In the winter

there are wildfowl by the thousand, including wigeon, pochard and tufted duck; in the summer there are great crested grebes and dabchicks; and in the spring and autumn, at migration time, all sorts of waders and seabirds stop over at the reservoir to rest and refuel on their arduous journeys.

A third of the Carsington shore is set aside as a conservation area, but the rest is accessible by footpath, by bicycle and by horse. The main Visitor Centre is on the west shore, with an extensive car park (pay-and-display) off the B5035.

There are several mining villages to the north of Carsington Water, including Brassington, which boasts some fine 18th-century houses and a Norman church. Inside the church, look for the even older carving high on the west wall of the tower of a naked man with his hands on his heart.

Hopton village is now dominated by the reservoir, though there is a bypass for the main road. Until 1989 Hopton Hall (not open) was the home of the Gell family, who made their

Insight

THE RUDDY DUCK

One of Carsington Water's controversial residents is the American ruddy duck. Just 50 years ago this little duck (it has a big blue bill, white cheeks, a reddish back and a stiff tail) was quite unknown outside the Wildfowl Trust, but it escaped and is now so widespread that it is threatening to overrun Europe, diluting the genes of its close relative, the European white-headed duck, in the process.

fortune from the nearby limestone quarries and made their name as scholars, politicians and travellers. Along the limestone rise to the north runs the Hopton Incline, once the steepest gradient for any standard-gauge railway line in Britain, using fixed engines and cable-haulage to set the High Peak Railway on its journey from Cromford Wharf to Whaley Bridge. It is now the High Peak Trail. Further north again is the Via Gellia, a road created and named by one of the Gells, through superb, flower-rich woodland along a valley west of Cromford.

DOVEDALE

Fame, beauty and availability are a heady mix. Dovedale's Stepping Stones appear on a thousand postcards and attract a million visitors, all of whom seem to be queuing to cross the crystal waters of the Dove at the same time. The National Trust does a heroic job to manage this part of its South Peak Estate, but it is perhaps a good idea to keep away from the place on sunny Sundays.

The Dove flows for 45 miles (72.4km), but only a short section of it is called Dovedale; above the Viator Bridge it becomes Mill Dale, then Wolfscote Dale and then Beresford Dale. But it is to the gorge of Dovedale that the visitors flock, for within the space of a few miles of easy riverside walking, on a broad level path, there are superb craggy rocks and pillars (all named) rising out of dense ash woodland, sweeps of open pasture, banks of flowers, dark caves and fine cascades of spring water. There is no road and only one main path, following the east (Derbyshire) bank. It is not even necessary to cross the stepping stones upstream from the car park on the Staffordshire side of the river, because there is a footbridge a few yards away.

Victorian fashion blighted Dovedale; it was praised by every famous romantic writer from Byron to Tennyson and was soon as popular as Switzerland. Donkey tours and guided expeditions once ferried people up the path to view the scenery. Of more enduring merit were the earlier words of Izaak Walton, who loved the Dove and put his head and heart into *The Compleat Angler*.

HARTINGTON

Hartington is a tourist honeypot but, like Tissington and Ashford, there is enough in the fabric and culture of

Insight

NATURE RETURNED

Just north of Carsington and Hopton, the landscape rises to a 1,000-foot (305m) contour, topped by a stone called King's Chair. This area is pockmarked by old lead mines and limestone quarries, but wild flowers abound on the open limestone and into the Via Gellia; in places several kinds of orchid jostle for space, and in ash woodland there are patches of the rare herb *Paris quadrifolia*.

the village to cope with popularity and still have a heart. Curiously, its heart is probably the duck pond, or mere, which sits like a round pearl in a circlet of duck-cropped lawn. Nearby is Ye Olde Cheese Shoppe, selling superb local Dovedale Blue. Just a stone's-throw away you will find tea rooms, a selection of shops, a pottery and two pubs – the latter were old coaching inns that hark back to the days when Hartington was a significant market town.

37

DOVEDALE

Insight

PLOUGHMAN'S PARADISE
The cheese shop at Hartington sells produce from the nearby Hartington Creamery, which was established in the 1870s and began making Stilton in the 1920s. The new owners sell an extended range of Peak District cheeses and many continue to come from local artisan cheese producers, including Dovedale Blue. The local pubs often sell beers brewed at the tiny Whim Brewery, based on a remote farm near the village. Truly a ploughman's dream come true!

One of the pubs has the unusual name, The Charles Cotton, after an angling resident of Beresford Hall, who happened to be the friend and collaborator of Izaak Walton. It was on the upper reaches of the Dove as it flowed below Beresford Hall that Cotton and Walton perfected their arts and gathered their fishing stories, published in 1653 as *The Compleat Angler*.

Just out of the village, up a steep side road to the east, is Hartington Hall, a sturdy yeoman's manor built in the 17th century. It was the home of the Bateman family but has been a youth hostel since 1934.

Also to the east of the village is a signal box of the Ashbourne–Buxton Railway, which closed in 1967 and is now an information centre on the Tissington Trail, while 3 miles (4.8km) north is Pilsbury Castle, now a mound, probably on the site of an Iron Age fort.

Hartington occupies a strategic position for walkers and explorers of the less obvious paths and byways. To the east and the west lie dry valleys and a lattice of green pastures and to the south is Beresford Dale.

ILAM
On most maps the River Manifold can be traced in a blue line, flowing south from Longnor to meet the Dove one mile (1.6km) below Ilam. In fact this is not usually what happens,

and, like several other celebrated rivers in limestone country, the Manifold has a secret life, flowing underground unless the water table is high. Below Wettonmill the river abruptly disappears and takes almost 24 hours to resurface, at the Boil Holes in the grounds of Ilam Hall. This explains why there are no footpaths along what appears on paper to be a pretty section of the lower valley. However, this does not mean the landscape is not interesting, but there is no clear focal point and the footpaths linking to the old halls of Throwley and Castern on the upper slopes of the valley are rarely walked.

Ilam, above the confluence of two famous rivers, has always been an important settlement, but never very large. Originally it belonged to Burton Abbey, but after the Reformation the estate was broken up among three families, the Ports of Ilam Hall, the Meverells of Throwley and the Hurts of Castern. Of these the Meverells no longer exist and Throwley Hall is a ruin; the Ports sold Ilam to Jesse Watts Russell in the early 19th century, and the Hurts continue to live at secluded Castern.

Alas, Russell swept away most of old Ilam and built a model village, the buildings of which have the look of a Swiss cuckoo clock. Ilam Hall was rebuilt on a grand scale; a quarter of it remains and is used as a youth hostel. The lovely parkland that surrounds it is open to the public. Close by is the church, totally rebuilt, but with two fragments from Saxon crosses and a Tudor chapel with a shrine to the local medieval hermit St Bertram.

The Ilam estate passed to the care of the National Trust in 1934 and the stable blocks and renovated Italianate gardens of Ilam Hall are a popular destination for day visitors. They are also drawn because of the pleasant parkland walks and partly because it is close to Dovedale and has literary associations – with Boswell, Johnson and Izaak Walton.

LONGNOR

The fate of little Longnor was sealed by the demise of the turnpikes and the lack of a railway link; its worthy ambition to be a proper market town withered away. It stands now in the no man's land that lies between the Manifold and the Dove, but at a pivotal point in the Peak District, in the very heart of the country. Around it are strip fields dating back to medieval times; just to the north lies Derbyshire and the limestone knoll country, while to the west are the darker gritstone hills of Staffordshire.

The Manifold at Longnor is no more than a babbling brook, but the valley is broad and dotted with meadows and sandstone barns. Yellowhammers and whitethroats sing from the thorn bushes; swallows swoop for insects over the reed grass. Longnor presides over the long, straight road like a drowsy cat over a barn floor. The village is pretty and compact, with a little square and a Victorian market hall.

There is a stone inscription above the entrance that carries the tariff of ancient market tolls.

MANIFOLD VALLEY

The Manifold and the Dove rise within a mile of each other below Axe Edge. As they head southeast together into limestone country, twisting and side-winding like pulled strands of wool, one is transmuted into a Staffordshire valley, the other into a Derbyshire dale. The difference in landscape terms is quite minimal; they both cut a course through superb scenery, meeting finally at Ilam, yet the Manifold Valley escaped all the Victorian hype and the more carnival atmosphere of Dovedale.

Wetton and Warslow villages, on the 1,000-foot (305m) contour on opposite sides of the valley, are the main access points for the most dramatic section of the Manifold. Neither makes very much concession to tourists, though both have good pubs (the Olde Royal Oak and the Greyhound). Warslow has a utilitarian look, as do its medieval iron stocks close to the school. It is an estate village of the Crewe family (of Calke Abbey, south of Derby) and lies at the very foot of the gritstone moors, which can be reached by taking the side road to the northwest. The village of Wetton is on the limestone, among dairy farms and barns, but its stout church and many of its cottages look as if they belong amongst heather.

A steep side road north of Warslow off the B5053 drops down to Ecton, and takes you to the start of the most beautiful section of the valley. It runs southwards along a thin strip of level meadow, with steep, flower-studded, almost alpine-looking, grassland banks.

The road, and what is now the Manifold Trail, follows the route of the Leek and Manifold Valley Light Railway, which opened in 1904 but only survived for 30 years; according to expert judgement it opened too late and closed too soon – if its odd Indian-style engines were still running today the line would make a fortune!

Close by to Wettonmill the Manifold usually disappears down swallow-holes, travelling all the rest of the way to Ilam underground. Meanwhile, the Manifold's tributary, the Hamps, heads southwards and the Manifold Trail stays with the old railway line, going along the Hamps to the large village of Waterhouses.

Once out of the depth of the valley, the steep limestone hill slopes are pockmarked with deep caves. The most famous and dramatic is Thor's Cave but several others, such as Ossom's Cave and Elderbush, have been explored or excavated and have produced bones and flints dating back to the Stone and Bronze Ages, when this was good hunting country.

All the domed hills, which are called Lows, are capped by cairns or barrows and it is very easy on the dry 'karst' hillsides to imagine yourself in another older world.

45

THOR'S CAVE, MANIFOLD VALLEY

SOUTHERN DALES

Insight & Visit

WELL DRESSING
The most famous of all the Peak District traditions, well dressing, probably has its roots in pagan ceremonies to placate water spirits. The Christian version has its origins at Tissington, where five wells ran with pure water during the Black Death. The villagers believed they owed their lives to the water, and dressed the tops of the wells as a sign of thanksgiving. Well dressing involves pressing flower petals, cones, seeds and fruits onto a clay base to create often a Biblical or local scene.

Activity

THE TISSINGTON TRAIL
This famous trail runs for 13 miles (20.9km) from Parsley Hay to Ashbourne, along the old railway line which closed in 1963. You will find the trail suitable for families and cyclists who appreciate a car-free countryside; it is possible to hire bikes at either Parsley Hay or Ashbourne, or bring your own and leave your car at the car park, on the old railway station.

TISSINGTON
Tissington is a real gem, and a gift to any photographer. The classic approach is off the A515, through a gateway and over a cattle grid, then along a drive lined with lime trees. The original avenue, of venerable pollards and tall standards, has recently been felled, but there are rows of young trees set further back. Into the village itself, past a walled yew and the first of several wells, sandstone cottages are set back behind wide grass verges and shaded by elegant beeches. The village has its village green, with the stream running through it, a duck pond complete with ducks, a Norman church and a grand Jacobean Hall. This is, and has been for centuries, an idyllic, well-managed estate village.

Tissington Hall, low and wide with mullioned windows and tall chimneys, is the home of the Fitzherbert family. It is set behind a low wall and gate of fine wrought ironwork (by Robert Bakewell).

SOUTHERN DALES

TOURIST INFORMATION CENTRES
Ashbourne
13 The Market Place.
Tel: 01335 343666
Hulme End
Manifold Valley Visitor Centre.
Tel: 01298 84679 (seasonal)

PLACES OF INTEREST
Derwent Crystal
Shawcroft, Ashbourne.
Tel: 01335 345219;
www.derwentcrystal.co.uk
Ecclesbourne Valley Railway
Wirksworth Station.
Tel: 01629 823076;
www.ecclesbournevalleyrailway.org.uk
High Peak Junction Workshops
Wirksworth.
Tel: 01629 822831
Original workshops, railway exhibition
and information centre.
Ilam Park
4.5 miles (7.2km) northwest of
Ashbourne. Woods and parkland
on the banks of the River Manifold.
Free but parking fees apply.

Middleton Top Engine House
Middleton Top Visitor Centre,
Middleton by Wirksworth.
Tel: 01629 823204
Engine house with a beam
engine to haul wagons up the
Middleton incline.
National Stone Centre
Porter Lane, Wirksworth.
Tel: 01629 825403;
www.nationalstonecentre.org.uk
Exhibition, guided walks and
gem panning.
Steeple Grange Light Railway
The Quarry Men's Line,
Middleton by Wirksworth.
Tel: 01246 205542;
www.steeplegrange.co.uk
Rides every ten minutes.
Wirksworth Heritage Centre
Crown Yard.
Tel: 01629 825225;
www.storyofwirksworth.co.uk
Former silk and velvet mill
with displays illustrating the
town's history.

54

SHOPPING
Ashbourne
Antiques shops in Church Street.
General market, Thu and Sat.
Wirksworth
General market, Tue.

LOCAL SPECIALITIES
Cheeses
Derbyshire and Staffordshire
cheeses (and bottled beers)
from Ye Olde Cheese Shoppe,
Hartington.
Tel: 01298 84935;
www.hartingtoncheese.co.uk
Crafts
Longnor Craft Centre,
The Market Hall,
Longnor.
Tel: 01298 83587
Honey
Daisybank Apiaries,
Newtown,
Longnor.
Tel: 01298 83526;
www.daisybankapiaries.co.uk
Peak District honey, mead.

Pottery
Rooke's, 1 Mill Lane, Hartington.
Tel: 01298 84650;
www.rookespottery.co.uk

SPORTS & ACTIVITIES
ANGLING
Fly Fishing
Carsington Water.
Tel: 01629 540478;
www.stwater.co.uk
BOAT HIRE
Carsington Water.
Tel: 01629 540478;
www.stwater.co.uk
CYCLING *SEE* **LONG-DISTANCE**
FOOTPATHS AND TRAILS
CYCLE HIRE
(For those marked P, website is
www.peakdistrict.gov.uk)
Ashbourne (P)
Ashbourne Cycle Hire Centre,
Mapleton Lane.
Tel: 01335 343156
Carsington Water
Tel: 01629 540478;
www.stwater.co.uk

SOUTHERN DALES

Middleton Top (P)
Visitor Centre,
Middleton by Wirksworth.
Tel: 01629 823204
Parsley Hay (P)
Peak District National Park
Centre, Waterhouses.
Tel: 01298 84493
Brown End Farm Cycle Hire
Brown End Farm.
Tel: 01538 308313;
www.manifoldcycling-brownendfarm.
co.uk
Manifold Valley Bike Hire
Earls Way,
Old Station Car Park.
Tel: 01538 308609;
www.visitpeakdistrict.com
GUIDED WALKS
Derbyshire Dales
Countryside Service
Planning and Development Services,
Town Hall, Matlock. Full guided walks
service. Tel: 01629 761326
National Park Walks with a Ranger
Peak District National Park.
Tel: 01629 816200;
www.peakdistrict.gov.uk

Peak District
Annual Peak District Walking Festival.
Guided walks April/May.
Tel: 0870 444 7275;
www.visitpeakdistrict.com/activities/
walking
Wirksworth & Peak District
Professional Blue Badge Guides.
Tel: 01629 534284
HANG-GLIDING
Airways Airsports
Ashbourne.
Tel: 01335 344308;
www.airways-airsports.com
HORSE-RIDING
Tissington Trekking Centre
Tissington Wood Farm,
Ashbourne.
Tel: 01335 350276
LONG-DISTANCE FOOTPATHS
AND TRAILS
The High Peak Trail
Follows the former High Peak Railway
from High Peak Junction (Cromford) to
Dowlow (south of Buxton). Derbyshire
Countryside Centre.
Tel: 01629 823204

Manifold Trail
Traces a former narrow-gauge railway from Hulme End to Waterhouses, 8.25 miles (13.3km) of walking or cycling. Visitor Centre at Hulme End.

The Tissington Trail
Part of old Ashbourne–Buxton railway. Runs for 13 miles (21km) alongside Dovedale from Ashbourne and joins the High Peak Trail near Parsley Hay. Derbyshire Countryside Centre. Tel: 01629 823204

WATERSPORTS
Carsington Water, Near Ashbourne. Tel: 01629 540478

ANNUAL EVENTS & CUSTOMS
For the full programme visit www.visitpeakdistrict.com

Ashbourne
Shrovetide Football, Shrove Tue–Ash Wed. Highland Gathering, with parade of pipe bands, mid-Jul. Ashbourne Show, late Aug. Well dressing (Wyaston & Mayfield), mid-Jun.

Bonsall
Hen racing, The Barley Mow pub, early Aug. Well-dressing, Jul.

Dovedale
The Dovedale Dash, a 4.25-mile (6.8km) cross-country run which starts on Thorpe Pastures, early Nov.

Hartington
Well dressing, Sep.

Ilam
Manifold Valley Agricultural Show, The Arbour, Castern Hall Farm, early Aug. Dovedale Sheepdog Trials, mid-Aug.

Longnor
Well dressing and Wakes, early Sep. Longnor Races, Sep.

Tissington
Well dressing, Ascension Day. World Toe-Wrestling Championships, (Bentley Brook Inn), Jun.

Wirksworth
Well dressing, late May. Clypping of the Church service, early Sep. Festival of Music and Arts, Sep.

TEA ROOMS

Bassett Wood Farm
Tissington, Ashbourne,
Derbyshire DE6 1RD
Tel: 01335 350254
www.bassettwoodfarm.co.uk
This friendly, welcoming and informal
tea room set in a working farmhouse
is always heady with the rich aroma of
home-baking. Look out for local jams,
honey and dairy produce and indulge
in tasty ice-creams.

Beresford Tea Room
Market Place, Hartington,
Derbyshire SK17 0AL
Tel: 01298 84418
This tea room is also the village post
office. As ever, local produce and local
baking is to the fore; try some of the
local Dovedale Blue (maybe on a chilli
oatcake). In the winter months, the
hotpot is particularly welcoming.

Craft Centre Coffee Shop
Longnor Market Hall, Longnor,
Staffordshire SK17 0N
Tel: 01298 83587
This enterprising little café serves
a variety of home baked produce
including Staffordshire oatcakes.
The little Victorian Market Hall is
also home to locally made art and
crafts, all for sale.

Manifold Tearooms
Ilam Hall, Ilam,
Staffordshire DE6 2AZ
Tel: 01335 350245
The stable block to the Hall
(a youth hostel) is now a National
Trust tea room with an emphasis on
vegetarian and organic foods. Enjoy
tea and cakes or try one of the more
substantial meals. The local cheeses
are also good.

ERRWOOD RESERVOIR

Buxton & Western Moors

BUXTON

CHAPEL-EN-LE-FRITH

THE GOYT VALLEY

LEEK

LYME PARK

MACCLESFIELD

THE ROACHES

WHALEY BRIDGE

WILDBOARCLOUGH

INTRODUCTION

Macclesfield and Leek mark the western and southern edges of the Peak uplands. To the north are Whaley Bridge and Chapel-en-le-Frith and in between are dramatic gritstone outcrops and windswept heather moors. Two rivers drain the watershed: to the north the Goyt, rising on the peaty slopes of the Cat and Fiddle Moor; to the south the pretty River Dane. To the east of all this is the grand spa town of Buxton.

ESSENTIAL SIGHTS

Unmissable attractions

Leek, which was built on the silk industry, is where the first hills of the Peak District rise up from the Staffordshire Plain. These heights are known as the Staffordshire Moorlands and are marked by outcrops, such as the Roaches and neighbouring Ramshaw Rocks and Hen Cloud. Unsurprisingly, they are very popular with hang gliders and rock climbers. By contrast, the elegant spa town of Buxton lies at the centre of the Peak. Its many buildings of note include the Royal Crescent and the Opera House. Opposite the Crescent is St Ann's Well, the source of Buxton's famous heated spa water and nearby is the awesome gulf of Poole's Cavern, the Peak's most accessible cave for intrepid explorers.

1

1 Errwood Reservoir, Goyt Valley

It looks as if it has always been here, but this reservoir is a relatively recent addition to the valley landscape, along with its neighbour Fernilee. Built by Stockport Corporation, Fernilee was flooded in 1938 and Errwood followed in 1967. The Forestry Commission added woodlands in the 1960s. A fly-fishing club and a sailing club both make use of Errwood Reservoir.

2 Buxton

Situated in the Pavilion Gardens, on the banks of the River Wye, the impressive domed Octagon was first opened to the public in 1876. This magnificent glass and cast-iron structure today operates as a concert venue and also hosts antiques and collectors' fairs.

3 Whaley Bridge

The Peak Forest Canal ends at the picturesque Whaley Bridge canal basin. Colourful narrowboats and the tow path both provide a more leisurely way to explore this beautiful area.

Insight

THE BEST BREW

People still queue up at St Ann's Well in Buxton to fill plastic containers with the tepid water, claiming it makes the best tea in Britain. Try it straight from the well. It was good enough for Mary, Queen of Scots, and it was water that brought the Romans to the Peak District in the first place.

BUXTON

Dropping down from the high moors into the elegant spa town of Buxton, on the River Wye, is enough to make anyone blink in disbelief as they find themselves emerging out of the bleak wilderness into a bower of parks and gardens and grand Palladian-style buildings.

Through the centuries health resorts have sprung up in all sorts of unlikely places, and none more so than Buxton. The Romans, who had a passion for bathing, established a rest or leisure facility here in the days of Agricola, when the frontier fighting had shifted north to Caledonia and this was a safe haven with the additional benefit of natural warm springs. After the Romans left, the Christians came to take the 'cripple's cure' at St Ann's Well and to pray for miracles. By the 18th century Buxton, in common with other spa towns, was set firmly on the fashion trail.

The 5th Duke of Devonshire was responsible for the main building innovation at Buxton. He had been impressed in the 1770s by Bath's Royal Crescent and was awash with money from his Ecton copper mines. First he had the elegant semicircular Crescent built, complete with 42 pilasters and 378 windows, then the Great Stable with a central court and Tuscan columns, finally followed by Hall Bank and The Square, all built in a grand and imposing style. In the 19th century the 6th and 7th Dukes carried on the work, so that by late Victorian times the spa in the valley had completely eclipsed the old market town on the upper slope.

BUXTON

PAVILION GARDENS, BUXTON

Opposite the Crescent is the famous twin-domed old Pump Room, where smart visitors once took their prescribed mineral waters. Near by stands a modest fountain, which is the source of the famous waters and of Buxton's continued prosperity.

CHAPEL-EN-LE-FRITH

Unfortunately, a pretty name does not always describe a picturesque place. The frith, or forest, never really existed except to formalise a vast tract of Norman hunting preserve; most of the Derbyshire countryside was open ground rather than woodland.

The most obvious feature of Chapel-en-le-Frith today is its rather dowdy main road, which sweeps south into a hollow and on towards Buxton. A bypass now carries A6 traffic around to the east, but it will take some years for this part of Chapel to brighten up. However, turning off the main road at the white-painted Kings Arms at the top of the town, brings you directly

Insight

BRUTAL TIMES
One morbid episode in Chapel's history casts a long shadow. In the Civil War, following the Battle of Ribbleton Moor in 1648, 1,500 Scottish soldiers were imprisoned in the church for 16 days. The conditions must have been appalling. By the time they were let out, to start a forced march north, 44 men were dead. They were buried in the churchyard, a testament to brutal times.

to the market place and a change of character. Lovely cobbled paths and a medieval cross and stocks stand at the heart of the little square, overlooked by a café called The Stocks. Except on market day (Thursday) this is a quiet and out of the way place, perfect for a cup of tea and a wander.

Close by is the Roebuck Inn, and a little way further along the street, opposite the church, is the Bull's Head Inn, of which only the sign,

BUXTON & WESTERN MOORS

Insight

PEAK PANTHER

On a bright winter's day in 1995 a small group of birdwatchers saw something out of the ordinary. While wandering by the hedge along the western shores of Combs Reservoir they came across some large clawed footprints measuring 3.5in (89mm) wide, which were sunk deep into the mud. The prints didn't belong to a dog. After studying the photographs they had taken, it became obvious that a huge cat had been on the prowl – probably the infamous Peak Panther that has had may sightings in the hills above Chinley and Hayfield.

are hints of antiquity all around; the shaft of a Saxon cross, a weathered sundial and a view across what must have been glorious hunting country to the scenic crag-fringed edges of Combs Moss.

The village of Combs, just southwest of Chapel-en-le-Frith, has stone-built cottages centred on the welcoming Beehive Inn. A short walk away is Combs Reservoir, which has a sailing club and is also a popular spot for coarse fishing and birding.

THE GOYT VALLEY

The River Goyt meets the River Tame in Stockport to form the famous River Mersey. Its upper and middle reaches cleave a deep, gorge-like valley through some of the most accessible moorland in the Peak District. This is a great outdoor activity area that is threaded with plenty of by-roads, packhorse trails, as well as old railway tracks, a place where Cheshire meets Derbyshire amid a blaze of heather and bilberry-strewn uplands.

a wooden carved life-size shorthorn bull's head, still survives intact.

St Thomas à Becket Church stands on a grassy knoll overlooking a housing estate. The original chapel in the forest was built here around 1225, but was replaced in the early 14th century by a sturdier structure. Most of what is visible today is from the refurbishment of 1733, but there

The Goyt River flows from south to north; it rises on the slopes of Cat and Fiddle Moor, a wild and windswept place with a reputation for having the worst weather. The moor is named after the Cat and Fiddle Inn, at 1,690ft (515m) it is the second-highest pub in England. Like other high-altitude hostelries, such as The Snake or Tan Hill, it was built in the turnpike era at the start of the 19th century and is still a welcome sight for traffic on the sinuous A537. There are few other buildings to be seen for miles around, but some facilities are available at Derbyshire Bridge, which is the usual starting point to explore the Goyt Valley.

Years ago the Goyt was as natural an upland valley as is possible to exist in England, but the original scatter of ancient oaks has now been augmented or replaced by conifer plantations and the river and meadowlands were flooded to create the Fernilee and Errwood reservoirs. The combination of lake and forest, cobalt and viridian beneath the

Visit

GOYT'S MOSS

Below Cat and Fiddle Moor is Goyt's Moss, a colourful carpet of cotton grass and asphodel belying a treacherous surface of wet peat. In late April and May golden plovers and curlews add their voices to those of pipits and larks; this is also the breeding ground of the twite, a small finch with a pink rump.

magenta of heather moorland, rising to the highest point in Cheshire – at nearby Shining Tor, 1,834 feet (559m) – all help to make the Goyt a vividly colourful place.

Parking and picnic sites are dotted around the reservoir shores and the walks through the woodlands draw so many walkers and visitors that a one-way system was devised up the narrow road to Derbyshire Bridge. Be aware that at peak times, on summer Sundays and Bank Holidays, this road is closed to traffic.

81

LEEK

LEEK

The little Staffordshire mill town of Leek sits on a broad low hill in a bend of the River Churnet. Unlike most of the other towns circling the Peak District, Leek is not overshadowed by the hills and makes no extravagant claims to be an adventure centre. All around are green valleys and rolling pastures, full of grazing dairy cattle and longwool sheep.

To the south lies the Churnet, with a host of visitor attractions, such as the Caldon Canal, the Cheddleton Railway Centre and the old Cheddleton Flint Mill. To the southwest is Stoke-on-Trent with its fine pottery heritage. But to the north and east the foothills rise inexorably to heather moorland and limestone plateaux; like Macclesfield and Glossop there is a sense of a settlement butting as closely to the hills as it dared, exploiting the power of the elements. Textiles transformed Leek from a medieval market town to an industrial centre, but silk was the speciality, which meant that many of the early mills were small and clean, with better working conditions than those endured in the cotton mills of the Peak valleys. Most of the mill buildings are now put to other uses, but the wealth generated by silk is recalled in the many imposing buildings commissioned from the Victorian architects William and Larner Sugden.

The heart of old Leek, easily missed on a fleeting visit, is the cobbled-stone Market Place. At one end of it stands the 17th-century Butter Cross, a link with the town's dairying tradition. The cross was removed from its original location, at the lower side of the square towards Sheep Market, nearly 200 years ago and has since been restored. An attractive watermill stands at the edge of the town as a monument to James Brindley, the famous 18th-century canal engineer. Further upstream, a tributary of the Churnet was dammed to create Rudyard

Lake, to supply water for his Trent and Mersey Canal. A few miles north of the town, the Churnet itself has been dammed to form Tittesworth Reservoir. This site has many facilities including a visitor centre, woodland walks, car parks and a bird hide overlooking the shallow northern corner.

Insight

'SCHEMER' BRINDLEY

James Brindley, Leek's most famous son, was actually born at Wormhill, near Tideswell, but his family moved to Leek in 1726 when he was ten years old. He was apprenticed to a millwright at Sutton, near Macclesfield, when he was 17 and was soon solving all sorts of engineering problems. Most of his ideas worked, and he was nicknamed 'Schemer'. Wealth and notoriety followed, but in his later years he became famous for his canal designs, particularly the Trent and Mersey and its Harecastle Tunnel. Brindley died from pneumonia in 1772.

LYME PARK

Lyme Park (National Trust) on the western edge of the Peak District is a modest mirror image of Chatsworth. The imposing Hall is a leading example of the Palladian style, the work of the Italian architect Giacomo Leoni in the 1720's; it featured as 'Pemberley' in the 1995 BBC adaptation of *Pride and Prejudice*. The interior, a heady mix of Elizabethan and later rooms, houses remarkable Mortlake tapestries and the Lyme Caxton Missal prayer-book.

Lyme was the home of the Legh family for 600 years and has sufficient style to make it one of the top visitor attractions in the area, set in a rural idyll of gardens, parkland and moorland, yet only a stone's throw from Stockport.

Those who prefer outdoor attractions to the splendours of the stately home will enjoy the wildfowl on the lake and herds of red and fallow deer among the trees. The 1,300-acre (520ha) park

LYME PARK

also has excellent short walks and viewpoints: a modest alternative to the high hills if the weather is closing in.

MACCLESFIELD

The town of Macclesfield sits firmly at the foot of the hills, close enough to suffer draughts of frost-laden air and share any low cloud. Specialising in silk was its salvation but also its downfall. From a market town, Macclesfield first became known for buttons, then for all kinds of silken products. By the mid-19th century the town was bursting at the seams, with 56 silk 'throwsters' (producing the thread or thrown silk) and 86 businesses creating silk fabric or finished goods. Despite this success, or perhaps because of it, the workforce lived in wretched conditions, with an appalling level of infant mortality, and with nowhere to go when the industry hit one of its frequent declines.

Silk mills, chapels and banks – solid square buildings of blackened stone – are scattered through the town today. Among them is the huge Sunday School on Roe Street, which is now a heritage centre with a silk museum and shop. Near the old market cross, behind St Michael's Church and its beautiful soot-covered chapel of 1501, lies a narrow garden terrace known as Sparrow Park (officially, the Broadhurst Memorial Gardens). This is a pivot of the old town, a place to stop and ponder its rich and chequered history. Below the gardens there is a steep bank, down which run the picturesque 108 Steps. There is a view through the shrubs of the railway station and over the hinterland of the town, to green remembered foothills at the western face of the Peak.

On the farmland of the foothills, above Sutton Lane Ends and a growing patchwork of housing estates, lie the two Langley reservoirs. Both places were excavated in the mid-19th century to provide clean water for Macclesfield.

89

TRENTABANK RESERVOIR, MACCLESFIELD

Activity

TEGG'S NOSE AND THE GRITSTONE TRAIL

The best introduction to the Cheshire slice of the Peak landscape is from Tegg's Nose Country Park, along Buxton Old Road to the east of Macclesfield. There are superb views from the Windy Way car park and walks along a network of tracks and pathways, by the old quarry or down through woodland to the reservoirs above Langley. It is possible at this point to join the Gritstone Trail, a waymarked footpath running the length of Cheshire from Lyme Park to Mow Cop.

This was in response to infant mortality and disease among the mill workers. But young Charles Tunnicliffe, the famous country artist, knew them in more peaceful times as a haunt of sandpiper and moorhens. Further into the hills are Ridgegate and Trentabank reservoirs, the winter resort of pochard and goldeneye; Cheshire's largest heronry is also here. Then comes the conifer blanket of Macclesfield Forest, once part of a vast royal hunting forest. Close to Trentabank is a Forest Visitor Centre, from where there are walks and drives. At the eastern edge of the forest lies the tiny Chapel of St Stephen, where a rush bearing ceremony takes place each August. At the highest southern access point there is a path that leads onto open moorland and up to Shutlingsloe, a distinctive Peak summit.

About 3 miles (4.8km) south of Macclesfield is Gawsworth Hall, a fine Tudor black-and-white manor house, which was the birthplace of Mary Fitton. This renowned lady is thought by some to be the 'Dark Lady' of Shakespeare's sonnets, who aroused such emotional turmoil in the poet. We shall probably never know, but the house is worth a visit anyway, for its wonderful old timberwork, its paintings and its suits of armour. The grounds, thought to be a rare example of an

MACCLESFIELD CANAL

Elizabethan pleasure garden, include a tilting ground and are the venue for open-air theatre and craft fairs during the summer months.

THE ROACHES

There are few real peaks in the Peak District (the name is derived from the Old English pecsaetan, meaning hill-dwellers), but the most elegant and craggy-topped are in the far west: Hen Cloud, Ramshaw Rocks and The Roaches. They are gritstone outcrops, similar to those in the Dark Peak and Eastern Moors, but here they were more heavily contorted or squashed together, leading to a landscape of misfit valleys, steep slopes and rock faces rather than plateau moorland.

Ramshaw Rocks are probably the best-known outlier of the Roaches, because they tower above the roadside on the A53 north of Leek and have a face-like formation. The A53 and the quiet winding roads to the west of Axe Edge lead to some interesting places.

95

Insight

BEYOND THE LAW

Below Cut-thorn Hill lies Three Shires Head, where a packhorse bridge stands at the cusp between Derbyshire, Cheshire and Staffordshire. Many years ago, this was where illegal prizefights took place because the local police forces had no authority to pursue suspects beyond their own county boundary. For the very same reason, Flash became the capital of coin counterfeiting, and the word Flash ('Flash Harry', 'flash money' etc) entered the language to denote a fake.

Axe Edge itself is too high to be anything but wild. One notable village tucked away just off the main road is Flash, claimed to be the highest village in England at 1,518 feet (462m). The River Dane rises nearby, jinking a course between hills and ridges and flowing southwest to Gradbach and Danebridge: this is delightful countryside full of trees and meadows, barns and cowslip banks. The Roaches ridge lies a few miles to the southwest of Flash and runs northwest to southeast, its main rock-climbing exposures facing the setting sun. A footpath follows the crest of the ridge, links with Back Forest and creates a 4-mile (6.4km) ridge walk with superb views. Heather clothes the upper hills, bracken and woodland the slopes. The area has become famous as the home of a colony of red-necked wallabies, a Tasmanian oddity that arrived at a private zoo at Swythamley Hall in the 1930s and escaped to form a wild population.

WHALEY BRIDGE

The little town of Whaley Bridge grew up with dust on its face and Goyt water in its veins. Coal and textiles provided the only gainful work – both long gone. These days there is hardly a whisper of this past and employment is more varied. Visitors call on route to visit the Goyt Valley or the Peak Forest Canal.

THE ROACHES

BUXTON & WESTERN MOORS

TOURIST INFORMATION CENTRES
Buxton
The Pavilion. Tel: 01298 25106;
www.visitbuxton.co.uk
Leek
Market Place. Tel: 01538 483741;
www.discoverstaffordshirepeakdistrict.
com
Macclesfield
Council Offices, Town Hall.
Tel: 01625 504114;
www.peaksandplains.co.uk

PLACES OF INTEREST
Brindley Mill
Mill Street, Leek. Tel: 01538 483741;
www.brindleymill.net
Buxton Museum and Art Gallery
Peak Buildings, Terrace Road.
Tel: 01298 24658
Cheddleton Flint Mill
Leek Road, Cheddleton.
Tel: 0161 408 5083. Free.
Chestnut Centre
Castleton Road, Chapel-en-le-Frith.
Tel: 01298 814099;
www.ottersandowls.co.uk
Otter haven, owl sanctuary.

Churnet Valley Railway
Cheddleton Station,
Churnet Valley Railway.
Tel: 01538 360522;
www.churnet-valley-railway.co.uk
Dunge Valley Hidden Gardens
Windgather, Kettleshulme.
Tel: 01663 733787;
www.dungevalley.co.uk
Hare Hill Gardens
4 miles (6.4km) north of
Macclesfield off B5087.
Tel: 01625 584412
Lyme Park
Disley. Tel: 01663 762023;
www.nationaltrust.org.uk
Macclesfield Silk Heritage
Heritage Centre, Roe Street.
Tel: 01625 613210
Pavilion Gardens
Buxton. Tel: 01298 23114. Free.
Poole's Cavern
Green Lane, Buxton. Tel: 01298 26978;
www.poolescavern.co.uk
Silk Museum & Paradise Mill
Park Lane, Macclesfield.
Tel: 01625 612045;
www.macclesfield.silk.museum

West Park Museum
Prestbury Road, Macclesfield.
Tel: 01625 619831

FOR CHILDREN
Blackbrook Zoological Park
Winkhill, nr Leek. Tel: 01538 308293;
www.blackbrookzoo.co.uk
Blaze Farm
Wildboarclough. Tel: 01260 227229;
www.blazefarm.com
Freshfields Donkey Village
Wormhill Road, Peak Forest.
Tel: 01298 79775. Donation requested.
www.donkey-village.org.uk
Rudyard Lake Steam Railway
Tel: 01995 672280;
www.rlst.org.uk

SHOPPING
Buxton
Market, Tue and Sat.
Chapel-en-le-Frith
Market, Thu.
Leek
Market, Wed and Sat.
Macclesfield
Outdoor market, Tue, Fri, Sat.

LOCAL SPECIALITIES
Farmers' Markets
Buxton, first Thu.
Leek, 3rd Sat each month.
Macclesfield, 3rd Fri each month.
Whaley Bridge, 2nd Sat each month.
Spa Water
Spa water from the fountain in
The Crescent, Buxton.

PERFORMING ARTS
Buxton
Opera House, Water Street,
Buxton. Tel: 01298 72190;
www.buxton-opera.co.uk

SPORTS & ACTIVITIES
ANGLING
Fly
Danebridge Fisheries,
Wincle.
Tel: 01260 227293
Errwood Reservoir,
Goyt Valley.
Tel: 01663 734220
Lamaload Reservoir,
Macclesfield.
Tel: 01625 619935

103

BUXTON & WESTERN MOORS

Coarse
Combs Reservoir, Whaley Bridge.
Tel: 01663 762393
Rudyard Lake. Tel: 01538 306280;
www.rudyardlake.com
BOAT HIRE/SAILING
Rudyard Lake
Tel: 01538 306280
Tittesworth Reservoir
Tel: 01782 722226;
www.peakpursuits.co.uk
**COUNTRY PARKS AND
NATURE RESERVES**
Grin Low and Buxton
Country Park, Buxton.
Tegg's Nose Country Park,
Macclesfield. Tel: 01625 614279
Tittesworth Reservoir.
Tel: 01538 300400
CYCLING
Macclesfield Forest
On and off-road routes.
Rudyard Lake, near Leek
Level cycling trail on old
railway beside Rudyard Lake.
The Middlewood Way
Runs northwards from
Macclesfield to Marple.

CYCLE HIRE
Parsley Hay
Parsley Hay Bike Hire.
Tel: 01298 84493
GUIDED WALKS
Professional Blue Badge Guides.
Tel: 01629 534284
Buxton
From Tourist Information Centre.
Tel: 01298 25106
Etherow–Goyt Walks
Etherow Country Park.
Tel: 01614 276937
Leek
Town walks from Leek
Tourist Information Centre.
Tel: 01538 483741
Peak District
Annual Peak District Walking Festival.
Guided walks.
Tel: 0870 444 7275;
www. visitpeakdistrict.com/walk
Walking the Bollin Valley
Tel: 01625 534790
National Park Walks with a Ranger
Peak District National Park.
Tel: 01629 816200;
www.peakdistrict.gov.uk

HANG-GLIDING
Leek
Peak Hang Gliding Centre,
8 Whitfield Street, Leek.
Tel: 07000 426465;
www.peakhanggliding.co.uk
HORSE-RIDING
Buxton
Buxton Riding Centre, Fern Farm.
Tel: 01298 72319;
www.fernfarmcottages.co.uk
Flash
Northfield Farm Riding & Trekking
Centre, Flash. Tel: 01298 22543;
www.northfieldfarm.co.uk
**LONG-DISTANCE FOOTPATHS
& TRAILS**
The Gritstone Trail
35 miles (56km) from Disley in
Cheshire to Kidsgrove in Staffordshire.
The Middlewood Way
11-mile (18km) trail between
Macclesfield and Marple.
The Midshires Way
230 miles (370km) Stockport to Bucks.
The Pennine Bridleway
350 miles (563km) from Cromford to
Byrness (Northumberland).

ANNUAL EVENTS & CUSTOMS
For the full programme visit
www.visitpeakdistrict.com
Well dressing in Chapel-en-le-Frith,
Buxworth, Peak Forest and Buxton, Jul.
Buxton
Antiques Fair, May.
Brass Band Festival, May.
Buxton Festival, Jul.
Buxton Fringe Festival, Jul.
International Gilbert & Sullivan
Festival, Jul/Aug.
Country Music Festival, Sep.
Cheddleton
Carnival, Aug.
Flash
Teapot Parade, Jun.
Well dressing, mid-Jun.
Leek
Leek Arts Festival and Carnival, May.
Leek & District Show, Jul.
Macclesfield
Sheep Dog Trials, Aug.
Macclesfield Forest
Rush-bearing ceremony, St Stephen's
Church, Aug.

105

TEA ROOMS

Brookside Café
Wildboarclough, Macclesfield,
Cheshire SK11 0BD
Tel: 01260 227632
Popular with ramblers and cyclists
in this corner of the Peak District,
the Brookside has been offering
sustenance for more than 40 years.
Expect great home-cooking, from
afternoon teas to wholesome meals,
served amid stunning countryside.

The Coffee Shop
Lyme Park, Disley,
Cheshire SK12 2NX
Tel: 01663 762023
In the shadow of Lyme Hall, this
unpretentious and welcoming place
offers simple, filling fare. There's
a more extensive restaurant in
Lyme Hall itself.

The Coffee Tavern
Shrigley Road, Pott Shrigley,
Bollington, Cheshire SK10 5SE
Tel: 01625 576370
This is a firm favourite with walkers,
cyclists and diners in these western
fringes of the Peak District. Here you
can enjoy anything from a modest pot
of tea and a cake or a light snack to a
three-course meal.

Roaches Tea Rooms
Paddock Farm, Upper Hulme,
Leek, Staffordshire ST13 5SE
Tel: 01538 300345
www.roachestearooms.co.uk
A very homely place at which to indulge
in that local delicacy, the Staffordshire
oatcake (a dream with bacon and
cheese), cream teas, calorific treats or
maybe just a mug of tea, enjoying the
remarkable scenery of The Roaches.
The friendly folk at Paddock Farm cater
for walkers and climbers.

106

BUXTON

THE GOYT VALLEY

BAKEWELL

The Hanging Gate
Meg Lane, Higher Sutton,
Macclesfield, Cheshire SK11 0NG
Tel: 01260 252238
Open fires, gnarled beams, country-cottage décor, exemplary food, beers from Hydes brewery; a heady mixture.

Navigation Inn
Brookside, Buxworth, High Peak,
Derbyshire SK23 7NE
Tel: 01663 732072
www.navigationinn.co.uk
Enjoy fine real ales from far and wide and tasty, traditional English cooking. Its comfy restaurant and the most time-honoured of bars make this an unmissable destination.

Quiet Woman
Earl Sterndale, Buxton SK17 9SL
Tel: 01298 83211
No music here, just the hum of conversation over home-made pork pies washed down with Marstons and guest beers. Behind the pub is a smallholding with friendly stock to keep the kids entertained.

The Ship Inn
Wincle, Cheshire SK11 0QE
Tel: 01260 227217
This pub clings to the steep side of the Dane Valley above superb woodlands and the enticing ridges and clefts of the western Peak. Just two little rooms provide shelter for happy drinkers of local beers and contented diners feasting on a superb menu strong on Cheshire produce.

The Swan Inn
Macclesfield Road, Kettleshulme,
Whaley Bridge, Cheshire SK23 7QU
Tel: 01663 732943
Under new ownership this tiny pub is a champion of local beers, complementing the range of largely locally sourced food. It's the perfect place to unwind after a good walk.

White Peak

INTRODUCTION

Bakewell is the mid-point of the Peak District and through it runs the River Wye: downstream is the fine medieval mansion, Haddon Hall. Upstream the river quickens as the valley narrows surrounded by limestone hills. Little side valleys twist their way through the fossil seabed. Water often flows far below the ground, so that in past centuries village folk relied on wells, and gave thanks each summer for their constancy. The White Peak is a land of drystone walls and beautiful dales, of crouched churches and good pubs.

112

ASHFORD IN THE WATER

Unmissable attractions

The pale limestone plateau of the White Peak is criss-crossed by miles of drystone walls and dissected by steep-sided dales. It is a walkers' paradise with 1,600 miles (2,575km) of public footpaths crossing wild moor, along river banks or past sleepy villages. It is also crossed by the Tissington, High Peak and Monsal trails: former railway lines now converted to cycling and walking routes. Bakewell is the only town within the Peak District National Park and is celebrated for its famous pudding. Just downstream is the romantic medieval pile of Haddon Hall, frequently used as a film location.

1

1 Monsal Dale
A narrow footbridge spans the waters of the River Wye in Monsal Dale. Stop off at Monsal Head, above the valley (there is a large car park) to admire the far-reaching views of the dale and the river down below.

2 Ashford in the Water
Nestling on the banks of the River Wye, Ashford in the Water is one of the most attractive of the Peak villages. It is well known for its colourful Blessing of the Wells procession, which takes place annually on Trinity Sunday.

3 Bakewell
The original Bakewell Pudding was the result of a culinary misunderstanding between the local innkeeper and her cook. However, the recipe was such a success that a Mrs Wilson, wife of the local Tallow Chandler, started making the puddings for sale from Bakewell from 1860.

115

ASHFORD IN THE WATER

ASHFORD IN THE WATER

Only 2 miles (3.2km) from Bakewell and just off the busy A6, it is a wonder that Ashford in the Water has kept any kind of dignity. In fact it is one of the most attractive and interesting of all the Peak villages, sited on a twist of the River Wye, on the ancient port but bypassed today by the new road. Grassland and the A6 have taken the place of the 'black marble' quarry works on the approach to the village. 'Black marble' was an impure limestone that turned shiny black when polished; it was popular in Victorian times (for vases, fire-surrounds, and so on) and the works were extensive and probably represented the only blot on the Ashford horizon. This is not to say there had not been industry in the village before Henry Watson established his marble works in 1748. It simply means the scale was different. Many of the wonderful stone houses and cottages on the main triangle of lanes served as workshops when they were built; there was a corn mill, a candle-maker and several stocking mills. The community was more varied and the buildings more eccentric, and this has left a distinctive character to the place today, part pretty English village, part quirky Derbyshire jumble.

At the middle of Ashford is a green space, called Hall Orchard, once part of the grounds of Neville Hall, a medieval hunting lodge that stood on the eastern side. The space is now a playing field but there are some tall trees, notably limes, and around the rest of the village fine ash trees to offer shelter and shade. 'Oak won't grow in Ashford' goes the local saying, and this has proved true over the years.

On Church Street, between the Hall Orchard and the Wye, is a 17th-century tithe barn (now a private house) and the parish church. Most of the structure of the church is Victorian but just above the porch, returned to its original position, is a Norman tympanum. The Normans

117

Visit

VIRGIN CROWNS

In Ashford church hang four 18th-century virgin crants, or crowns. These were funeral garlands, carried at maidens' funerals and then hung on beams or from the roof of the church. They are made of white paper attached to a wicker frame, and in the middle is a paper glove, bearing the name of the girl. The tradition of virgin crowns was widespread across England, but rarely do any of the fragile garlands survive to tell the sad tale.

were not as expert as the Saxons at carving animals so there is some doubt about what the stone slab depicts. It may be a tree of life with a boar on one side and a lion on the other, or it may be meant to represent the Royal Forest with a boar and a wolf.

The main attraction for visitors to Ashford is the river, crystal clear and full of trout. There is space to wander along the banks, and three

bridges, two of which are old. Close to the cricket field the bridge on the closed road carries an inscription 'M. Hyde 1664'; the brief memorial refers to The Reverend Hyde, who was thrown from his horse here and drowned. Upstream, on an old packhorse trail, is the attractive Sheepwash Bridge; a stone fold on one side shows where the sheep were held before being plunged into the river and made to swim across to clean their fleeces.

Southwest of Ashford, on the dry-limestone plateau, is Sheldon, a small lead-mining village close to the famous Magpie Mine. The main shaft of the mine was 728 feet (222m) deep and water had to be pumped up to a sough, which carried it to the Wye on the curve below Great Shacklow Wood. In 1966 the roof of the sough collapsed and there was an explosion of pent-up mud and rocks. The resulting debris can still be seen today; the floodwater was gone all too quickly in a tidal wave. Over the years

ASHFORD IN THE WATER

BAKEWELL

Ashford has grown quite used to being flooded – 'in the Water' was added to the name quite recently.

BAKEWELL

Bakewell is always busy with visitors and locals. Its streets are never free of traffic and bustle, but if you accept this from the outset there's every reason to enjoy the town; it is an exciting mixture of old and new, a tourist honeypot that is still thrives as a working community.

There are surprisingly few very old buildings considering the rich history of Bakewell (it was granted a market and 15-day fair in 1254), but there are a number of fine 17th-century structures, such as the Market Hall, which serves as the Peak District National Park Information Centre, and the Town Hall. Up the steep road on the west side of the town stands an airy grass-covered knoll on which sits the lovely parish church of All Saints. Like many of the churches in Derbyshire it is broad and low, but

Insight

BAKEWELL PUDDING

The fame of the humble Bakewell Pudding has spread so far that it is now high on the list of favourite British puds. According to tradition, the recipe was the result of an error that emanated from the kitchen of the Rutland Arms Hotel in around 1860. The cook, flustered perhaps by a special order to prepare a strawberry tart for some very important guests, put the jam in first, then poured in the egg mixture designed for the pastry on top. Far from being a disaster, the new invention was hailed as a culinary triumph and became a regular item on the menu. Incidentally, don't ask for a Bakewell Tart in the home of their origin – they are always known here as 'puddings'. And please don't enquire who has the original recipe, included in the will of the cook at the Rutland Arms – it is still the cause of local dispute and rivalry!

Visit

TROUT WATCHING

One of the idlest pleasures on rivers like the Wye is to stand on a bridge and watch trout keeping stationary against the current below. Swimming against the flow looks remarkably easy, if you have the fins for it. Brown trout, with spotted flanks, are the native game fish made famous by *The Compleat Angler*; the rainbow trout is an American import, able to tolerate warmer and more polluted water.

with a spire as sharp as a 3H pencil. Inside you will find there are some fascinating fragments of Saxon and Norman stonework, and the famous monument to Sir John Manners and his wife Dorothy, who are reputed to have eloped together from Haddon Hall in 1558. Outside the hall stands the shaft of a 9th-century stone cross, beautifully decorated with vine scrolls and figures. Near by the church is The Old House and Cunningham Place, a 16th-century

parsonage now a museum. Monday is market day in Bakewell, when cattle and sheep wagons converge behind Bridge Street and the market place is decked with awnings. Escaping the bleating and banter is very easy; the River Wye runs alongside, and within a few seconds it is possible to be out of the crowd and feeding ducks or trout along the river. Upstream is one of the oldest bridges in England, built in about 1300; impossible to appreciate if you are driving over it but a scene-stealer from water level where its five arches and solid breakwaters are visible. In the distance stands Castle Hill, where the settlement of Bakewell began in AD 920 with the establishment of a Mercian fort.

EYAM

Disease was a fact of life in medieval England and many of the Peak villages suffered the horrors of Black Death and plague. What made the weaving village of Eyam special was the attempt by the local

EYAM

Insight & Visit

GEOLOGY OF THE PLAGUE VILLAGE

Exploring the upper pathways of the village, such as the grassy alley from the Royal Oak up Little Edge and along May Walk, it is obvious that Eyam lies on the very edge of the limestone and only just qualifies as a White Peak village. In fact, most of the houses sited on the north side, towards Eyam Edge, were constructed using sandstone, which was the preferred building material, whilst the greyer, less durable limestone was used a few hundred yards away to the south. Just across the valley, and – perhaps understandably – rarely mentioned in tourist guidebooks, you can see two great working quarries, ripping into the hills for road-stone.

rector, William Mompesson, to keep the outbreak in 1665–66 within the confines of the community and not let it be carried elsewhere. The whole village was put in quarantine, entire families tragically perished and Eyam became a byword for tragedy and self-sacrifice. According to tradition, the plague virus was introduced into the village by a tailor called George Viccars, who bought some infected cloth from London. He died a few days after arriving at Eyam, lodging with Mary Cooper at what is now called Plague Cottage. A fortnight later Mary's son Edward died and the whole community braced itself. The young rector quickly sent his own children away, but stayed with his wife to care for the sick and organise the quarantine. Over the months, through 1665 and into the autumn of 1666, about 250 people died, including Mompesson's wife, but the heroic efforts of the village were successful and the epidemic did not spread outside Eyam.

Some of this plague story has surely been embellished in the telling, but the essential details are there, recorded in the parish register, among the gravestones around St Lawrence's Church and on nearby cottages. Towns such as

Derby and Chesterfield probably suffered worse epidemics of bubonic plague; Eyam has kept its unique place in history because you can stand beside victims' homes, read about their lives and look across to see their graves.

Eyam today is neither a sad place nor dwelling in the past. It stands on the hill brow between Middleton Dale and Eyam Moor, as self-contained and aloof as ever. Visitors are impressed by the fine Saxon cross in St Lawrence's churchyard and come to Eyam to enjoy the traditional well dressing and the sheep roast. But folk-memories of the plague still send a shiver down the spine.

HADDON HALL

Close your eyes and imagine a rambling family castle, built with style, English to the core, unchanged for centuries, full of ghosts, set among trees and pastures above a clear meandering river. What you have in mind is probably Haddon

Insight & Visit

HERALDIC BEASTS

Important and aristocratic families always had their own ancestral emblems or devices, which accounts for the curious animal shapes that appear on the gutters and in the ironwork of Haddon Hall. The boar emblem represents the Vernon family and the peacock the Manners family; they appear together all over the estate, most spectacularly as carefully clipped and maintained topiary figures in the huge yew bushes outside the gardener's cottage.

Hall. It is the single most impressive and authentic building in the Peak District, the one that turns historians into poets. Why is this? The simple explanation is that the building is a perfectly proportioned medieval manor house, which has been hardly touched since the 16th century. The rest is down to its history, romantic atmosphere and imagination. Haddon Hall was originally owned by the Vernon family from 1170 to 1567.

125

HADDON HALL

LATHKILL DALE

The house came to the Vernon family by marriage and passed to the Manners family in the same way. Over all those years the house was extended gradually; the Peveril Tower in the 12th century, the cross-wing in the 14th, battlements in the 15th, a gatehouse and courtyard in the 16th and the Long Gallery early in the 17th century. But after that it was left to slumber while the Manners family moved to the magnificent Belvoir Castle as Dukes of Rutland.

Thus the house escaped the fickle architectural fashions of the 18th and 19th centuries, but it was not neglected – it was meticulously maintained, so that when the 9th Duke (then the Marquis of Granby) began his restoration of Haddon in the early 20th century, his task was by no means daunting. The duke ensured that as much as possible of the original structure should be preserved, and that any replacements were carried out to the highest standards.

Haddon Hall reflects a sense of history today that can only come from remaining in the same family for over 800 years. Whether Dorothy Vernon really did escape down the long staircase, out from the chapel to the packhorse bridge to elope with her lover John Manners in 1558, is still a subject for speculation, but perfectly in keeping with the romance of the place.

LATHKILL DALE
The classic farmscape of silver-green pastures criss-crossed by drystone walls is dramatically disrupted on the White Peak plateau by the Derbyshire Dales, a series of steep-sided valleys in the limestone. The best dales are gathered together to form a National Nature Reserve, and the jewel in the crown is Lathkill Dale, which runs eastwards from the village of Monyash to the River Wye below Haddon. Access to Lathkill Dale is from Monyash or Over Haddon, which lies 2 miles (3.2km) southwest of Bakewell.

LATHKILL DALE

WHITE PEAK

From the west the dale starts out dry, but between Ricklow and Cales Dale the River Lathkill rises out of a cave and soon broadens out into a beautiful, crystal-clear stream, the haunt of water voles and dippers. Unlike the pasture and silage fields of the plateau, the grassland of the dale is ablaze with wild flowers. The rabbit-cropped south-facing slopes sparkle with rockrose and trefoil, which attract blue butterflies and burnet and forester moths. The shaded herbage of the north-facing slopes is the habitat for one of the Dales' specialities, Jacob's ladder. Further down the Lathkill, following the now well-worn footpath towards Over Haddon, grassland gives way to scrub and to ash woodland that, in the early summer particularly, casts a translucent shade and is full of songbirds.

Lathkill Dale may look untouched, but for many centuries it was mined for lead. The shafts, drainage channels and spoil-heaps have been absorbed into the natural landscape to such an extent that they really enhance its natural beauty. Most of the lead had been exhausted by the 18th century but in the 1840s there was a grandiose attempt to drain the deep mines by building a steam engine, powered by a huge waterwheel fed by the Mandale viaduct. The scheme was, unfortunately, a disaster, as was the Over Haddon gold rush of 1894.

MILLER'S DALE

The River Wye rises at Buxton but then flows east to dissect the limestone plateau. Each reach of the river has its own character and each section of the narrow valley or dale has its own name. Thus Wye Dale turns into Chee Dale, which gives way to Miller's Dale, then Water-cum-Jolly Dale and Monsal Dale. They are names to conjure with and to stir the imagination.

The presence of the river is a unifying theme; it brought welcome industry to the outback in the days of the Industrial Revolution and around

132

PEAK FOREST

this industry the little settlement of Miller's Dale grew up, squeezed awkwardly into the narrow valley of the Wye. Here lived the rail men and quarry workers and their families, and there was even a station, but all of that is gone now and the industrial areas are returning to nature.

In many respects Miller's Dale, located on either side of Litton Mill, is the most impressive and complete dale to visit. Not only does the Wye negotiate a barrage of natural obstacles here, side-stepping hills, twisting through gaps and gorges and rock faces, but also there are mill races and weirs where the power of the water has been diverted to drive 19th-century cotton mills (Litton and Cressbrook, a little way further downstream). A recreational footpath, the Monsal Trail, runs the length of the dale, allowing access to the old mill yards (some of the buildings are still in use, but not for weaving). There are footbridges at either end of Miller's Dale allowing access to convenient car parks.

Several side dales run north from the main valley, often dry and grassy but sometimes decked with ash woodland and with a stream dancing down to meet the Wye. The most attractive are Cressbrook Dale, the best for wildlife and with some beautiful ash woodland, Tideswell Dale, with access to the village of Tideswell, and Monks Dale, close to the village of Wormhill. Wormhill belies its name by being an attractive scatter of old farmhouses, with a village green, stocks and a fountain/well (dressed in August) commemorating James Brindley, the famous canal engineer, who was born close by at Tunstead.

PEAK FOREST

High, wide and windswept, it is rather hard to believe that this landscape of sheep pasture was once a royal chase – the Forest in the Peak – or that its administrative capital was this little village. For about a century, until the relaxation of the Forest Laws in 1250, kings

135

Activity

WYE VALLEY VIEWPOINT

Pilhough Lane, going northeast out of Stanton, makes a pleasant walk or drive because of its superb views over the Wye Valley and Haddon Hall. Before the church was built parishioners had to walk this way to Rowsley, and the Thornhill family had a viewing platform, called the Stand or Belvedere, set into the steep edge so that people could stop and rest and also enjoy the prospect.

managed the enclosure system and had premises in the Chamber, a building on the site of the present Chamber Farm. Swainmotes, or forest courts, settled any disputes. It was the foresters' task to care for the deer, by controlling grazing, by preventing walls from being built and by keeping people out. The deer increased fourfold, but this was only a temporary triumph. Around 1655 the land was allocated to the Dukes of Devonshire and was officially deforested, though the last of the trees had already been felled to provide pit props for the coal mines on Combs Moss. Scrub and heath took over the countryside until the turn of the 19th century.

and princes used the vast expanse of woodland and heath between the Goyt and the Derwent rivers as a private playground; they hunted wild boar and roe deer and stayed at the then recently built Peveril Castle, which stands high above Castleton to the northeast. By Elizabethan times most of the ancient woodland had disappeared, but what remained of the wilderness was fenced in as a deer park. A Steward and five Royal Foresters

The house called the Chamber of the Peak (which was built for the ranger) and the few cottages that made up the village, had been the heart of the royal forest, but had not stood among trees; this part of the limestone plateau was known as the Great Pasture and was used for sheep, as it still is today.

MOCK BEGGAR'S WALL

TIDESWELL

sweet-chestnut trees. The initials WPT, carved into the lintels of many doorways, refer to William Thornhill, who built most of the village in the 1830s and whose family lived at Stanton Hall. The 18th-century Flying Childers Inn celebrates the greatest racehorse of its day, trained by Sir Hugh Childers for the 4th Duke of Devonshire. Opposite the inn is Holly House that still has half of its windows still blocked up to avoid the 1697 window tax.

Birchover Lane, running south of Stanton, follows the western edge of the moor. Parking places give access to pathways through birch scrub and over heather and bilberry to the Bronze Age landscape. About 70 barrows or burial cairns have been identified on the small island of gritstone found here. The biggest, covering the site of twelve cremations, still stands 5 feet (1.5m) tall, inside a double ring of stones with an outer diameter of 54 feet (16.4m). There are also three stone circles or monument, the most famous is the Nine Ladies. Outside this stone ring, about 100 feet (30.5m) to the south, stands the solitary King Stone, which is part of the ritual site. The legend has it that a fiddler and nine maidens were turned to stone for dancing on Sunday. This is a typical example of prehistoric culture becoming Christianised.

TIDESWELL

Daniel Defoe, searching for the famous 'Seven Wonders of the Peak' in 1726, was not impressed by the ebbing and flowing well he viewed in a garden of Manchester Road in Tideswell. This may have been because he was looking at the wrong well (the original 'Wonder' was probably at Barmoor Clough), but in any case the water no longer ebbs and flows with the tide and Tideswell got its name from an ancient British chieftain called Tidi. This is not to say that wells were not important in the village; it lies at the 1,000-foot (304m) contour on the limestone

TIDESWELL

plateau, set in a dry bowl amid a grey cobwebbing of walls and wind-scorched fields. In fact, Tideswell is renowned for the quality of its well-dressing ceremony, which starts the Wakes Week on the Saturday nearest Saint John the Baptist's Day (24 June); the week's festivities are concluded with a traditional torchlight procession and a unique Morris Dance.

In the 14th century Tideswell was a thriving place, confident in the future of the wool trade and lead mining. The parish church, dedicated to Saint John the Baptist, reflected this optimism; it was built in just 75 years and is a classic cruciform shape, of Decorated and Perpendicular styles, spacious and with superb fittings, carvings and brasses. That Tideswell dwindled to a village was in some ways a stroke of luck, particularly as the glorious church, often described as the 'Cathedral of the Peak', was bypassed by rich patrons and Victorian megalomaniacs, and

stands today in splendid unaltered isolation. Around the church, the largest one in the area, run lawns and railings separating it from the more prosaic buildings at the heart of the village.

Two of Tideswell's renowned musical forefathers are buried in the church: 'the Minstrel of the Peak', William Newton, who died in 1830, and Samuel Slack, who died in 1822. Slack, whose name bore no relation to his vocal chords, was famous for two things: singing for George III and for stopping a bull dead in its tracks by bellowing at it. His voice, apparently, could be heard over a mile (1.6km) away.

To the east of Tideswell is the little village of Litton, a pretty gathering of 18th-century cottages beside a green with a set of stocks close to the Red Lion pub. Tideswell Dale and Cressbrook Dale run south, from west and east of the village, beautiful in their own right as well as giving access to Miller's Dale on the River Nye.

WINSTER

Midway between the sleepy little villages of Elton and Wensley (which has its own Wensley Dale, but no cheese) rests the sleepy little village of Winster. It lies off the main tourist routes, so you need to make a detour, though it is close enough to Matlock to make use of its shops and services. Most of the attraction of Winster is its characterful history, as one of the old lead-mining centres with 18th-century houses lining the main street between a fine 17th-century Dower House (now a hotel) and a 15th- to 16th-century Market House. The latter is matchbox-sized and a delightful structure of weathered stone arches, once open but now bricked in to keep it all standing, and an upper floor of brick, which may have replaced its earlier timbers. The National Trust bought the Market House in 1906, its first acquisition in the Peaks, and part of it houses an Information Centre. Close by is Winster Hall, an early Georgian house said to be haunted.

Activity

A HERMIT'S CAVE NEAR ELTON

West of Winster is the old lead-mining village of Elton. A popular walk heading north from the village leads to a small medieval hermit's cave at Cratcliffe Rocks – carved into the cave is a crucifix. An unusual rock formation known as Robin Hood's Stride and a stone circle are also seen on this walk of about 4 miles (6.4km).

Visit

CRESSBROOK DALE

Cressbrook Dale, just to the south of Tideswell, is part of the Derbyshire Dales National Nature Reserve. You may see wild orchids, cranesbill, mountain pansy, globeflower and spring sandwort growing on the limestone grassland in abundance. One of the many alkaline-loving plants is the Nottingham catchfly, which loves dry, stony places. The white flowers roll back in daytime, but are fragrant at night with perfume designed to attract pollinating moths.

ARBOR LOW'S ANCIENT STONES

WHITE PEAK

Visit

ARBOR LOW'S ANCIENT STONES

Three miles (4.8km) along the Long Rake west of Youlgreave, off the road to the left and accessible from a car park, is the famous henge of Arbor Low, probably built by the Beaker People in around 2000 BC. The whole monument, with rock-cut ditch, bank and a circle of 47 stones, measures 250 feet (76.2m) across. Although the massive stone blocks are all lying flat and half buried, Arbor Low is still a powerful place, especially in winter sunlight.

Winster used to be full of alehouses; witness the name Shoulder of Mutton, carved by the door of what is now a private house on West Bank. At the top of the bank, just out of the village, is the still-thriving Miners Standard, which has on display some of the old lead-mining equipment. It is here that the traditional Winster Morris dancers perform their flamboyant dances at the start of Wakes Week in June each year; a

procession then leads through the village, finishing up at the Miners Standard for refreshment.

A later tradition is that of pancake races on Shrove Tuesday. It began as light-hearted fun, organised by the local headmaster as a diversion during wartime for the children, but has now become a more serious but still fun race, with secret training and stringent rules about making the batter.

YOULGREAVE

A long, handsome village on the shoulder of Bradford Dale, Youlgreave (known as Pommie by most locals) has one of the most elaborate well-dressing ceremonies in the Peak District, taking place at Midsummer each year, when five wells are dressed with biblical scenes. The White Peak tradition has its roots in the days when wells were essential and were blessed to give thanks for water. However, in the case of Youlgreave, the records only go back to 1829, coinciding with the

148

provision of the village's own public water supply via a conduit from the Dale below. The water was gathered in a huge circular stone tank called The Fountain, which stands in the middle of the village. Nearby, on the opposite side of the street, is the Co-op building, which once had a vital role in the social survival of the area but is now a youth hostel.

On the east side of Youlgreave, by the road which then sweeps down to Alport, stands All Saints Church, described by experts as one of the most impressive churches in Derbyshire. Essentially Norman and with an unusually broad nave, the most obvious feature of All Saints is its 14th-century tower, chunky and stylish in the best Perpendicular tradition. Inside are sturdy columns and a 13th-century font, unique in that it has two bowls, and the fine monuments include a tiny effigy of Thomas Cokayne, who died in 1488. The church was restored in 1870 and has stained-glass windows by Burne-Jones and Kempe.

Insight

DEW PONDS
Dew ponds are a feature of limestone pastures in the White Peak. Because the underlying rock is porous there are no natural pools, so farmers have created their own, filled by rain, mists, dew and hosepipes.

Three bridges cross the River Bradford below Youlgreave, including a clapper bridge of stone slabs and a packhorse bridge, now a footbridge. The short walk to the confluence with the Lathkill is popular, but by turning southeast, over the main bridge and on to the Limestone Way, you can explore the fine countryside towards Birchover, past the Iron Age hill-fort of Castle Hill and the Nine Stones Close Circle (four stones are still standing tall), to the great tumbling rock tors of Robin Hood's Stride (once known as Mock Beggar's Hall), Cratcliffe Rocks and on Rowtor Rocks.

149

WHITE PEAK

TOURIST INFORMATION CENTRE
Bakewell
The Old Market Hall,
Bridge Street.
Tel: 01629 816558

PLACES OF INTEREST
Arbor Low Stone Circle
Upper Oldhams Farm, Monyash.
Cascades Gardens
Bonsall.
Tel: 01629 822813;
www.derbyshiregarden.com
Some 4 acres (1.6ha) of
themed gardens.
Eyam Hall
Tel: 01433 631976;
www.eyamhall.com
The furniture, portraits and other items
at the Hall reflect the fact that this is
still a family home and has been for
centuries. Also home to a craft centre.
Eyam Museum
Tel: 01433 631371;
www.eyammuseum.demon.co.uk
The museum tells the story of the
bubonic plague, how it reached Eyam
and was contained there.

Haddon Hall
Bakewell.
Tel: 01629 812855;
www.haddonhall.co.uk
A splendid house that has
remained virtually untouched
by the passage of time.
Topiary gardens.
Old House Museum
Bakewell.
Tel: 01629 813642;
www.oldhousemuseum.
hammerdesign.co.uk
This Tudor house is home to a folk
museum and a Victorian kitchen; toys
and lace are among the exhibits.
Stanton Moor
Nine Ladies Stone Circle.
Winster Market House
Winster, 4 miles (6.4km) west
of Matlock.
Tel: 01335 350503;
www.nationaltrust.org.uk
Restored by the National Trust, the
Market House is now used as an
information centre. The building dates
back to the late 17th/early 18th century.
Free.

150

SHOPPING
Bakewell
Market on Mon, includes cattle, except
Bank Holiday Mon when a general
market is held.
LOCAL SPECIALITIES
Bakewell Puddings
Original Bakewell Pudding Shop,
The Square, Bakewell.
Tel: 01629 812193;
www.bakewellpuddingshop.co.uk
Bloomers Original Bakewell Puddings,
Water Lane, Bakewell.
Tel: 01629 814844
General Foodstuffs
Bakewell Farmers Market,
last Sat of month.
Foods from The Chatsworth Estate,
Chatsworth Farm Shop, Stud Farm,
Pilsley, Bakewell.
Tel: 01246 583392

Meats
New Close Farm Shop,
Over Haddon, Bakewell.
Tel: 01629 814280;
www.newclosefarm.com
Home cured pork, bacon and
cooked meats.
Pork Pies
Connoisseurs Deli,
Water Street, Water Lane,
Bakewell.
Tel: 01629 812044

WHITE PEAK

SPORTS & ACTIVITIES
GUIDED WALKS
Bakewell & Peak District
Professional Blue Badge Guides
can arrange walks for individuals
or for parties. Tel: 01629 534284.
Derbyshire Dales Countryside Service
Planning and Development Services,
Town Hall, Matlock. Full guided walks
service. Tel: 01629 761326 for details.
National Park Walks with a Ranger
For more details contact the Peak
District National Park.
Tel: 01629 816200;
www.peakdistrict.gov.uk
Annual Peak District Walking Festival
Large programme of guided walks in
late Apr/early May.
Tel: 0870 444 7275;
www.visitpeakdistrict.com/walk
Peak Walking Adventures
Tel: 07870 778585;
www.peakwalking.com
HANG-GLIDING
Bradwell
Derbyshire Flying Centre.
Tel: 0845 108 1577;
www.d-f-c.co.uk

HORSE-RIDING
Haddon House Riding Stables
Over Haddon, Bakewell.
Tel: 01629 813723;
www.haddonhousestables.co.uk
LONG-DISTANCE
FOOTPATHS & TRAILS
The Limestone Way
A 46-mile (74km) route south
from Castleton through the
White Peak to Rocester
(Staffordshire).
The Midshires Way
Stretches 223 miles (360km) from
Stockport to Buckinghamshire
via the White Peak.
The Monsal Trail
Runs for 8.5 miles (13.7km) from
Blackwell Mill Junction near
Buxton to Coombs Viaduct
near Bakewell.
NAVIGATION SKILLS
Tideswell
Jaret House, Queen Street,
Tideswell
Tel: 01298 872470;
www.silvanavigationschool.com
Map and compass training.

ANNUAL EVENTS & CUSTOMS

For the full programme visit
www.visitpeakdistrict.com

Ashford in the Water
Well dressing, late May, early Jun.
Blessing of the Wells Trinity Sunday,
May.

Bakewell
Well dressing, late Jun/early Jul.
Carnival, early Jul.
Bakewell Show, early Aug.

Bradwell
Well dressing, early Aug.

Eyam
Well dressing, late Aug.
Plague Commemoration Service,
last Sunday in Aug.
Carnival, Aug/Sep.

Flagg
Point-to-Point races, first Tue
after Easter.

Little Longstone
Well dressing and demonstration,
mid-Jul.

Litton
Well-dressing demonstration, mid-Jun.
Well dressing, late Jun/early Jul.
Litton Horticultural Show, early Sep.

Middleton by Youlgreave
Well-dressing demonstration, late May.
Well dressing, late May/early Jun.

Monyash
Well-dressing demonstration, late May.
Well dressing, late May/early Jun.
Antiques and Collectors' Fair, late Aug.

Pilsley
Well dressing, mid- to late Jul.

Stoney Middleton
Well dressing, late Jul.

Tideswell
Wakes Week, late Jun.
Well dressing, late Jun/early Jul.
Male Voice Choir and Silver Band
Annual Concert, early Jul.

Winster
Pancake racing, Shrove Tuesday.
Winster Wakes Festivities,
late Jun/early Jul.

Wormhill
Well dressing and demonstration,
late Aug.

Youlgreave
Well dressing, late Jun.

TEA ROOMS

Eyam Tea Rooms
The Square, Eyam,
Derbyshire S32 5RB
Tel: 01433 631274
At the Town End part of Eyam and
overlooking the pretty square this tea
room has a particular reputation for
fine home-made cakes, gateaux and
scones. There's also a good choice of
vegetarian meals and snacks.

Monsal View Café
Monsal Head, Ashford in the Water,
Derbyshire DE45 1NL
Tel: 01629 640346
Overlooking magnificent Monsal Dale
this friendly, stone-floored café with a
roaring fire in winter offers filling fare,
from snacks to restaurant meals and
Derbyshire cream teas.

**The Original Bakewell
Pudding Shop**
The Square, Bakewell,
Derbyshire DE45 1BT
Tel: 01629 812193
 www.bakewellpuddingshop.co.uk
Above the shop where Bakewell's
famed recipe was re-created, this
comfortable tea room has exposed
beams reminiscent of a medieval barn.
Indulge in sandwiches and pastries,
afternoon tea to a more filling meal,
but don't miss out on a generous
helping of Bakewell Pudding.

The Old Smithy Tea Rooms
Church Street, Monyash,
Derbyshire DE45 1JH
Tel: 01629 810190
www.oldsmithymonyash.pizco.com
Set beside the village green and
ancient cross, the Old Smithy provides
supremely well for walkers and visitors
to this delightful old village. Although
renowned for its all-day breakfast,
traditional cream teas and pastries
are its main draws.

HADDON HALL

MONSAL DALE

The Red Lion
Litton, near Tideswell,
Derbyshire SK17 8QU
Tel: 01298 871458

Tiny beamed rooms, uneven stone floors and glowing logs in the hearths make this inn a magnet for pub aficionados. A friendly landlady, affable locals, great microbrewery beers and a very tasty menu make it one of the best in the Peak District.

The Bull's Head Inn
Foolow, Derbyshire S32 5QD
Tel: 01433 630873

A row of cottages in a peaceful hamlet forms this classic inn. The cosy interior features beams, flagstone floors, oak panelling, log fires and simple furnishings. To one end there is a smarter dining room; space here, then, for walkers, diners and locals to partake of the beers from the Peaks Ales Brewery with the guarantee of good, filling fodder, including grand Sunday roasts.

The Lathkil Hotel
Over Haddon, Bakewell,
Derbyshire DE45 1JE
Tel: 01629 812501
www.lathkil.co.uk

This long-established inn was built to serve lead-miners. Today's guests tuck into a mix of simple bar meals, top-notch dishes, and beers from Peak District breweries.

The Barrel Inn
Bretton, Eyam, Derbyshire S32 5QD
Tel: 01433 630856
www.thebarrelinn.co.uk

Derbyshire's highest pub, The Barrel Inn stands right on the lip of Eyam Edge, giving immense views across the heart of the White Peak. Expect a selection of beers from Hardys and Hansons brewery and good size portions of tasty, but unpretentious pub food, served in comfortable surroundings of antique seats, age-smoothed flagged floors, low beams, country prints and brass plates.

CURBAR EDGE

Derwent Valley & Eastern Moors

BASLOW

CALVER & CURBAR

CHATSWORTH

CHESTERFIELD

CRICH

CROMFORD

DARLEY DALE

THE DERWENT DAMS

GRINDLEFORD

HATHERSAGE

MATLOCK

INTRODUCTION

A ribbon of high gritstone moorland runs all the way from Stocksbridge in the north to Matlock in the south, which serves as a buffer between the industries and suburbs of Sheffield and Chesterfield and the main artery of the Peaks, the River Derwent. At the edge of the heather moors are great shelves of gritstone, etched by ancient ice into a famous series of west-facing cliffs or Edges. At the head of the Derwent there are many attractive villages, all quite different, and several historic houses, of which Chatsworth House stands supreme.

160

DERWENT VALLEY

ESSENTIAL SIGHTS

Unmissable attractions

Watched over by Froggatt, Curbar, Baslow and Stanage edges, the Derwent flows down from the northern Peak District, winding through a mellow valley, skirted by woods, meadows and pretty villages. On the river banks is the magnificent Chatsworth House. Joined by the Wye, the Derwent flows on through a narrow gorge where the little town of Matlock has been built. Overlooked by the cliffs of the Heights of Abraham, Matlock is a tourist honeypot. Old Matlock is on the east bank of the Derwent, where the turbulent waters are ideal for whitewater rafting and kayaking.

1

3 Crich Tramway Village
A fascinating place where visitors can ride on vintage trams, which run from a period street setting into open countryside.

1 Calver & Curbar
The little village of Calver nestles in the Derwent Valley beneath rugged Curbar Edge, an area popular with both walkers and climbers.

2 Chatsworth House
Standing within superb parkland and fine gardens, Chatsworth House, often known as the 'Palace of the Peak', is a treasure trove of works of art.

BASLOW

The 18th-century turnpike road from Sheffield used to cross the River Derwent next to St Anne's Church in the oldest part of Baslow, called Bridge End. A modern bridge now spans the river a short distance to the south, making it possible to idle about the 17th-century triple-arched bridge and take a closer look at the little toll house (the doorway is just 3.5 feet/1m high) that guards it. Further along the lane on the west bank of the river stands Bubnell Hall, which is as old as the bridge, while on the east bank, above the main road, stands Baslow Hall, an early 20th-century copy that has been converted into the luxurious Fischer's Hotel. On the far side of Baslow is Nether End, almost a village in itself, gathered around its own little Goose Green and with a row of pretty thatched cottages, which overlook Bar Brook. Thatched cottages are now quite rare in the area, although 'black thatch' (heather or turf) may once have been more widespread. Nether End marks the north entrance to the Chatsworth Estate and there is a touch of sophisticated comfort about everything; this applies equally to the nearby Cavendish Hotel, which contains some fine antiques from Chatsworth.

Further east along the Sheffield road the Bar Brook cuts a nick in the dramatic gritstone scarp, with Baslow Edge on one side and Birchen Edge on the other. A sea of bracken laps the footings of the rock faces, while the moorland above the Edge is a lonely wilderness of heather and the home of merlin and grouse. It was once the home of farmers too, in the Bronze Age, when the climate was a little kinder. It is astonishing to find field systems still visible from more than 3,000 years ago. Below Baslow Bar, just out of Nether End, it is also possible to see narrow fields separated by drystone walls that follow the old reverse-S pattern, the sign of ox-ploughing in medieval times.

CALVER & CURBAR

The Derwent divides these shrinking communities; Calver on the west bank lies in the lee of the limestone hills, while Curbar sits below a gritstone edge, close to the moors. A bridge built in the 18th century links them, but this is bypassed by a crossing just downstream and most people never notice Curbar as they swing west to Calver Sough.

Calver has an industrial side to its character; shoes and sinks were among its products. The steel sink factory occupies what was once a cotton mill, built by Richard Arkwright in 1805 and employing up to 200 people. The mill's moment of glory came in the 1970s when its satanic profile won it the role of Colditz Castle in a television series.

On the other side of the Derwent, Curbar is a quiet place on the shoulder of pastureland before Curbar Edge. The older features of the village include a circular pinfold or stock-pound, a covered well and circular trough and a lock-up with a conical roof. These structures survived because they were fashioned in stone and were built to last.

The old Chesterfield turnpike heads east out of Curbar, seeking the gap in the gritstone edge on the skyline. Great stone slabs were easily won from the Edge and were used in the area for more than just millstones. On the tussocky pasture close to the village lies a small group of gravestones marking the final resting place of the Cundy family, who died of the plague in 1632 (more than 30 years before the Eyam outbreak). Further up, several natural slabs of rock bear biblical references, the work of a molecatcher-cum-preacher, Edwin Gregory, who worked on the Chatsworth Estate a century ago. Finally, as the road straightens and heads southeast over the Bar Brook, there are drystone walls, guideposts and a clapper bridge, dating back to the packhorse era before the road became a turnpike in 1759.

165

CURBAR EDGE

Visit

CHATSWORTH DEER

The deer at Chatsworth are fallow deer, which were introduced into Britain by the Normans to grace their hunting forests. Fallow differ from the native red and roe deer in having a spotted coat and broad antlers. A visit to Chatsworth's glorious parkland can give the impression of an English version of the African Serengeti, with cattle, sheep and deer instead of wildebeest and impala.

CHATSWORTH

Towards the end of the 17th century, William Cavendish, the 4th Earl of Devonshire and soon to be made the 1st Duke for his part in putting William of Orange on the throne, decided his house needed a radical new look. For a while he tinkered with alterations, but finally knocked everything down and started again. Demolishing one great historic house to build another might seem an odd investment of a lifetime, but in those days great families were judged by their homes and gardens; fashion and taste was everything.

The Chatsworth House that rose from the rubble of the Elizabethan mansion was of a classical, Palladian style, to the Duke's own design. It took about 30 years to complete and it set the seal on his new status – even some of the window frames were gilded on the outside. The irony is that he never saw it at its best. Great houses needed great gardens and grounds, and these took decades to establish. In the middle of the 18th century 'Capability' Brown and James Paine laid the foundations of what we see today by altering the course of the river and roads, building bridges and setting out woodland vistas.

Chatsworth House is bursting with great works of art in the most superb settings; the Painted Hall is a work of art in itself, with huge, swirling scenes from the life of Julius Caesar by Louis Laguerre on the ceiling and upper walls.

CHATSWORTH HOUSE

Activity

WILDLIFE OF THE MOORLAND

Of all the heather moorland in the Peaks the expanse above Beeley is probably the best for wildlife. This has been due in part to its isolation and lack of access, but now it is possible to explore several of its finest areas without damaging the most sensitive ecological sites. You don't have to walk very far to find the wildlife as the roadside walls are one of the best places to look. Lichen-coloured moths, such as the grey chi and glaucous shears, sit on the stone walls, while the full-grown caterpillars of emperor and northern eggar moths like to sun themselves on the tops of bilberry and heather clumps.

of the original village remains, called Park Cottage, but known at one time as Naboth's Vineyard. The biblical reference relates to the owner in 1838, who is supposed to have refused to sell or be relocated. Just one mile (1.6km) to the northwest lies Pilsley, more compact than

Edensor, with the Chatsworth Farm Shop, a pub and a microbrewery.

Just outside the Chatsworth Estate to the south, but within its influence and historic ownership, lies Beeley. This old working village, tucked neatly away and with many of the elements of a much older settlement, has quite a refreshing character. A tannery once stood beside the brook, and there was an estate-built school and a barn to house the coal wagons that supplied the Chatsworth Estate glasshouses with fuel. Over the years most of the old buildings have been put to other uses, but fortunately not the public house (The Devonshire Arms), which is still a good excuse for stopping on the way up to the moors.

CHESTERFIELD

The tall spire of St Mary's and All Saints Church would have tapered to an elegant pencil-point if its timbers had been properly seasoned.Instead it stands crooked and twisted, providing a unique landmark,

CHESTERFIELD

A.D. 1688.
IN A ROOM WHICH FORMERLY
EXISTED AT THE END OF THIS
COTTAGE (WHAT IS LEFT OF THE
OLD COCK & PYNOT) THE EARL
OF DANBY THE EARL OF DEVONSHIRE
AND MR JOHN D'ARCY (ELDEST SON
OF THE EARL OF HOLDERNESS) MET
SOMETIME IN 1688 TO CONCERT
MEASURES WHICH RESULTED IN THE
REVOLUTION OF THAT YEAR

CRICH STAND

famous for the wrong reasons. Medieval Chesterfield was a prosperous town of guilds; it aspired to have a church that was worthy of its status and was full of fine buildings. Many of these still exist behind shopfronts and occasionally appear when renovation takes place.

Chesterfield is an industrial town. Its heart still beats in time with the coalfields and it is worth visiting for its old inns and good humour. It lies outside the Peak District, but serves its eastern flanks and is a gateway from the M1.

To the north of Chesterfield lies the village of Old Whittington, where a group of daring conspirators led by the Earl of Devonshire met in 1688 to hatch a plot to overthrow the Catholic King James II. The plot was successful; the country welcomed William of Orange and the course of history was changed. The meeting took place in a little thatched inn called the Cock and Pynot, now known as Revolution House and a modest tourist attraction, furnished

in 17th-century style and with a video telling the story of the Revolution. Just 2 miles (3.2km) away is Newbold Moor, where the tiny Norman Chapel was attacked in the same year by a mob of Protestants. The chapel, now restored, has a simple weather-beaten charm. Near by is Tapton House, the home in later life of George Stephenson, the pioneer railway engineer.

CRICH

Perched atop a limestone anticline, the monument on Crich Stand glows from a distance looking like a lighthouse set on alabaster cliffs above a shadowy sea. Three beacon-towers have stood here, but each time they were destroyed by lightning strikes. The present structure dates from 1921 and is a memorial to the men of the Sherwood Foresters Regiment killed in the service of the Crown. The 63-foot (19m) tower is open to the public and offers fine uninterrupted views way out across eight counties.

177

BONSALL BROOK

DERWENT VALLEY & EASTERN MOORS

Visit

A CANAL NATURE RESERVE

Downstream of the Leawood aqueduct the Derwent Valley is particularly beautiful; in spring wild daffodils grow on the riverside pastures and the oak woods ring with the divine sounds of wood warblers, redstarts and pied flycatchers. Located just below Whatstandwell, the overgrown canal is a nature reserve, a haven busy with wildlife; frogs and grass snakes, dragonflies and kingfishers. Take the train to Ambergate and it's possible to walk along the tow path to the next station at Whatstandwell, where there is an excellent pub.

Cromford Canal was built in the early 1790s to link up with the Erewash Canal, which then ran southeast to Nottingham. Cromford Wharf marked its northern terminus, at the mill. A turnpike road was opened up in 1817, then in the 1830s the Cromford and High Peak Railway was constructed, which linked the Cromford Canal with the Peak Forest Canal at Whaley Bridge, thus linking the Trent with the Mersey. In its early years this busy 33-mile (53km) wagonway employed horses on the level stretches and steam winding engines on the inclines. It was considered an extension of the canals and the stations were called wharfs, but by the middle of the 19th century the age of steam had arrived and the Midland Railway was extended north from Ambergate to meet the High Peak line.

Arkwright's Cromford Mill is now undergoing an important restoration programme by the Arkwright Society, who aim to create a lasting monument to his extraordinary genius. There are guided tours and a visitor centre on the site interprets the mill's heyday. Cromford Canal is popular for family picnics and there is a tow path walk to High Peak Junction, where there is another visitor centre.

The Cromford and High Peak Railway closed in 1967 and is now a popular multi-use recreational trail,

184

the High Peak Trail (the new Pennine Bridleway follows it).

Cromford is made prettier by its large pond, behind the market square, and the Greyhound Hotel (built by Arkwright in 1778). The pond was originally one of the impounding reservoirs to hold water from the Bonsall Brook, but its margins are now the home of ducks and swans. On the other side of the A6, close to the wharf and within sight of Arkwright's elegant homes of Rock House and Willesley Castle, lies the old bridge and its ruined chapel, at the site of the 'crooked ford' that became Cromford.

DARLEY DALE

Four settlements along the Derwent were bound together under the name of Darley Dale a century ago, but the ties were never strong enough to give the place a corporate identity. The A6 has now taken over the railway as the nub of the community, leaving Darley with an artery but no heart.

Darley was the home of Sir Joseph Whitworth, the man who invented the screw thread. Munitions, which included a rifle that fired hexagonal bullets, nuts and bolts, and machine tools soon made him rich, and he bestowed much of his wealth on the local community by not only building a Whitworth Hospital but a Whitworth Hotel, a Whitworth Park and an Institute. Victorian benefactors liked to have their good deeds recognised, but in Whitworth's case his generosity won him few friends and he was not popular. Whitworth lived at Stancliffe Hall (not open), guarding his privacy behind high walls and hedges, and when he died in 1887 his dreams of a model village died too. Beside the A6 lies Stancliffe Quarry. Stone from here was sent to London, where it was used to pave Trafalgar Square and the Embankment. Below this, on the other side of the railway line and on a low mound above the river flats, is Churchtown on which stands the fine parish church of St Helens.

185

LADYBOWER RESERVOIR

Activity

'TIN TOWN'

Car parks and cycle hire make it easy to explore the western side of the Derwent Valley, along the shores of all three reservoirs and through the forest. By Derwent Reservoir and just south of Birchinlee the road passes beside the site of 'Tin Town', which was once a settlement of corrugated-iron houses provided for the navvies who built the upper reservoirs. For a decade at the beginning of the 20th century it was a self-contained community a thousand strong, with its own school and railway station; all that remains are a few grass-decked foundations and terraces.

last and largest, was inaugurated in 1945; as well as flooding 2 miles (3.2km) of the Derwent Valley this also spread up the Woodlands Valley, but not very far because there would be the risk of landslips. Ladybower now holds about 6,000 million gallons of water, the others slightly less; more than a third of the water

is piped to Leicester, another third to Sheffield, and the rest is shared between Derby and Nottingham.

Although the sheer scale of the engineering works is impressive, it is the creation of a Canadian-style landscape that draws visitors – big views over great sheets of water, curtains of mist and conifers decked in snow; definitely not very British, but a grand prospect. The forest looks dark and dreary, and there is no doubt that alien conifers are not a substitute for native oak when it comes to bio-diversity. Even so, there are a few surprises. Red squirrels keep a toe-hold here, and in good seed years the local chaffinches are joined by flocks of crossbills. Goshawks are widespread but furtive, except in the early spring when they soar high in display flight over the wooded cloughs.

The Derwent Dams are famous for their drowned villages; when there is a drought thousands of people flock to see a few uncovered stones. The only structure to

cheat the flood was the Derwent packhorse bridge, dismantled and rebuilt further up the valley to span the river at Slippery Stones. The legendary 617 Dambusters Squadron practised at Derwent Dams before their air raid on the Ruhr in 1943.

GRINDLEFORD

The best way to arrive at Grindleford is by train, either from the east, through the 3.5-mile (5.7km) Totley Tunnel (the second longest in the country) or from the west, back-tracking down the line from Hathersage along one of the prettiest silvan stretches of the Derwent. Before the advent of the Hope Valley line Grindleford was little more than a turnpike crossing (the toll house still stands, next to the bridge) and the nearby settlements of Upper and Nether Padley were small enough to be lost among the trees. However, the villages bloomed with the opening of the railway station in 1898; most of the houses jostling the slopes and terraces were built by the resulting wave of Sheffield commuters, but not so many houses that the villages merged or lost their backdrop of woodland.

Grindleford Station is actually in Upper Padley. A few hundred yards towards the Derwent, over Burbage Brook and past the converted watermill, lie the ruins of Padley Hall. Very little remains of the 14th-century mansion except the foundations. It was once the proud home of the Fitzherbert family, who were Roman Catholics and had the misfortune to be caught harbouring two priests at a time when it was illegal to celebrate Mass. In fact the timing could not have been worse; the Spanish Armada had set sail and the country was on the lookout for Papist spies. The two priests, Nicholas Garlick and Robert Ludlam (local men who had been trained in France), were taken to Derby where they were hung, drawn and quartered. As for John Fitzherbert, he died in the Tower 30 years later.

Padley Hall became the home of one of Elizabeth I's chief priest-catchers before becoming a farm. The gatehouse, which had survived as a barn, was restored in 1933 and is now a chapel; a pilgrimage in memory of the martyrs takes place each July.

In the other direction, following the Burbage Brook upstream, runs a lovely network of paths through Padley Gorge. The boulder-strewn slopes of the gorge are covered in a thick layer of mosses and ferns, thriving in the damp shadows of the ancient oak wood. The trees are sessile oaks rather than pedunculate oaks; the obvious difference is that the sessile acorns are 'sessile' and don't have stalks. Acorns are an autumn bonanza for birds and animals; badgers and squirrels, jays and woodpigeons all make the most of the easy pickings. The spring bonanza is the plentiful crop of caterpillars, gathered from the leaves by migrants, such as pied flycatchers and wood warblers.

Insight

HAUNTING REMAINS
Before World War II, Ashopton and Derwent, were small villages of stone-built cottages, but the building of the Ladybower Reservoir shattered the lives of the locals. After the completion of its dam in 1943 the reservoir gradually filled up and by 1946 was above the tops of the rooftops. The old gateposts of Derwent Hall still survive by the roadside and a noticeboard shows the positions of some of the original buildings in Derwent village, but after a dry spell the water level can sometimes fall sufficiently for you to see the crumbling walls and foundations of the village, surrounded by crazed drying mud.

Padley Gorge is part of the National Trust's Longshaw Estate. Longshaw Lodge, built as a shooting lodge for the Dukes of Rutland, stands beside the B6521 in attractive grounds. These are now the core of a country park, with access to the moorland above Froggatt Edge.

LADYBOWER RESERVOIR

Both these buildings stand beside the village green with its stocks; to the west stands the Vicarage, and to the east is Camp Green, the ramparts of a 9th-century stockade.

MATLOCK

Matlock is a tourist honeypot, but there is more to it than the fairy lights and family attractions. Old Matlock stands on the east bank of the Derwent, before it twists west, under the bridge. St Giles Church, the Rectory and Wheatsheaf House mark the original lead-mining settlement at the meeting of packhorse trails and turnpikes. Next door, Matlock Bath is the home of the Peak District Mining Museum, which incorporates Temple Mine, an old lead and restored fluorspar mine, with a self-guided tour that depicts its geology, mineralisation and mining techniques.

Matlock Bath started as a petrifying well and tufa quarry, but in 1696 a bath was cut into the encrusted limestone and a spa was born. In the 18th and early 19th centuries the cream of society took the waters, staying in fashionable hotels on the sides of the gorge. In 1849 the railway arrived and the place was swamped by day trippers.

Matlock Bank, built on the gritstone/shale terraces facing you as you cross the bridge from the south, grew up around a hydropathic spa in the 1850s; the spa was the brainchild of John Smedley, a local mill owner and it made use of soft water, for bathing in, rather than the thermal spring water available down the road at Matlock Bath. In the early 20th century there were 20 hydros on Matlock Bank and the steep streets had their own tram system.

Today, families come to the Matlocks to visit the popular Gulliver's Kingdom theme park, which is divided into five different worlds each offering many rides and attractions, or to take a cable car up to the Heights of Abraham, with its show caves, nature trail, water gardens and Fossil Factory.

MATLOCK BATH

DERWENT VALLEY & EASTERN MOORS

TOURIST INFORMATION CENTRES

Chesterfield
Rykneld Square.
Tel: 01246 345777/8;
www.visitchesterfield.info

Fairholmes
Upper Derwent Visitor Centre.
Tel: 01433 650953;
www.visitpeakdistrict.com

Longshaw Visitor Centre
Tel: 01433 631708

Matlock
Crown Square. Tel: 01629 583388;
www.visitpeakdistrict.com

PLACES OF INTEREST

Chatsworth House
Tel: 01246 565300;
www.chatsworth.org

Chesterfield Museum and Art Gallery
St Mary's Gate. Tel: 01245 345727;
www.visitchesterfield.info
Free.

Crich Tramway Village
Crich, Matlock. Tel: 01773 854321;
www.tramway.co.uk

Cromford Mill
Tel: 01629 823256;
www.arkwrightsociety.org.uk

Heights of Abraham
Matlock Bath.
Tel: 01629 582365;
www.heights-of-abraham.co.uk

The Herb Garden
Pilsley. Tel: 01246 854268;
www.theherbgarden.co.uk

High Peak Junction Visitor Centre
Cromford. Tel: 01629 822831

Lea Gardens
3 miles (4.8km) southeast
of Matlock, off A6.
Tel: 01629 534380;
www.leagarden.co.uk

Longshaw NT Visitor Centre
Grindleford.
Tel: 01433 637904

Nine Ladies Stone Circle
Stanton Moor. Free.

Peacock Information and Heritage Centre
Low Pavement,
Chesterfield.
Tel: 01246 345777
Free.

Peak District Mining Museum
The Pavilion, Matlock Bath.
Tel: 01629 583834;
www.peakmines.co.uk
Peak Rail
Matlock Station, Matlock.
Tel: 01629 580381;
www.peakrail.co.uk
Revolution House
High Street, Old Whittington.
Tel: 01246 345727
Free.
Sir Richard Arkwright's
Masson Mills
Matlock Bath.
Tel: 01629 581001;
www.massonmills.co.uk
Whistlestop Countryside Centre
Old Railway Station,
Matlock Bath.
Tel: 01629 580958
Free.
Working Carriage Museum
Red House Stables, Old Road,
Darley Dale.
Tel: 01629 733583;
www.workingcarriages.com

FOR CHILDREN
Chatsworth Farm and
Adventure Playground
Tel: 01246 565300;
www.chatsworth.org
Gulliver's Kingdom
Temple Walk,
Matlock Bath.
Tel: 01629 580540;
www.gulliversfun.co.uk
Matlock Bath Aquarium
and Hologram Gallery
110 North Parade.
Tel: 01629 583624;
www.matlockbathaquarium.co.uk
Matlock Farm Park
Darley Moor, Matlock.
Tel: 01246 590200
www.matlockfarmpark.co.uk

SHOPPING
Chesterfield
General market, Mon, Fri and Sat;
Flea market, Thu.
Matlock
General market, Tue and Fri.

TEA ROOMS

Bookshop Café
Scarthin Books, The Promenade,
Cromford, Derbyshire DE4 3QF
Tel: 01629 823272
www.scarthinbooks.com
Books, as well as on-site arts and
crafts exhibitions, draw the eye at
this quirky little vegetarian café in
Cromford. Home-bakes and tea bread,
pizzas, Fairtrade coffee, nine kinds of
tea and thick soups made from home-
grown vegetables are on offer.

The Country Parlour
Caudwell's Mill, Rowsley,
Derbyshire DE4 2EB
Tel: 01629 733185
The tea rooms, squeezed between the
River Derwent and the mill race, serve
scones, cakes and pastries baked on
site, many using flour milled next door.
Rest easy in old chapel seats and
pews, before visiting the craft centre
and the mill.

**The Grindleford Spring
Water Company**
Station Approach, Grindleford,
Derbyshire S32 2JA
Tel: 01433 631011
Known to generations of walkers and
cyclists, this venerable café is tucked
next to the west portal of Totley Tunnel,
on the Sheffield to Manchester line.
Enjoy the full breakfasts, snacks
and pint mugs of tea or coffee on
offer here.

Post Office Tea Room
Edensor, Derbyshire DE45 1PH
Tel: 01246 582283
This charming tea room is tucked away
just behind the village church and is an
integral part of the post office stores,
hidden amid the peaceful byroads of
the estate village. Expect quality cream
teas and dainties, snacks and soups,
many made using the Chatsworth
Estate produce.

CURBAR EDGE

MATLOCK BATH

The Devonshire Arms
Beeley, Derbyshire DE4 2NR
Tel: 01629 733259
www.devonshirebeeley.co.uk
This long-standing pub has everything
you'd expect from an old inn – beams,
flagstone floors and stone walls. Enjoy
the excellent food in the bar, snug or
restaurant, with good beers including
some which are brewed on the
Chatsworth Estate.

The Chequers Inn
Froggatt Edge, Calver,
Derbyshire S32 3ZJ
Tel: 01433 630231
www.chequers-froggatt.com
An old inn with a beer garden on the
outside, a chic dining pub within; the
best of both worlds is balanced. Expect
a smart interior of pastel-yellow walls,
polished floorboards and country-
cottage furniture. The first-rate menu
is to die for, bonuses are the real ales
and friendly staff.

The Strines Inn
Bradfield Dale, Bradfield,
South Yorkshire S6 6JE
Tel: 0114 2851247
This isolated inn is well worth the
adventure finding it. Nearly 500 years
old, its rooms ooze character, with
beams, nooks and crannies sporting all
sorts of bric-a-brac. You'll find good,
reliable pub grub, a clutch of real ales
and a beer garden with excellent views
across 'Little Switzerland'.

Yorkshire Bridge Inn
Ashopton Road, Bamford,
Derbyshire S33 0AZ
Tel: 01433 651361
www.yorkshire-bridge.co.uk
This rather lovely rambling place,
close to Ladybower Dam, has fires
and stoves to rid a winter's chill and
an award-winning flowery beer garden
to relax in on summer evenings.
The very wide and eclectic menu
(including a range of calorific sweets)
is supplemented by decent beers.

MAM TOR

Dark Peak

INTRODUCTION

Virtually every day large cloud banks menace the desolate summits of Bleaklow, Black Hill and Kinder. Snow is almost as likely in June as in January; rain is inevitable. This is high country with a bed of millstone grit lying just beneath the peat; on the surface is a skim of bog moss or cotton grass and it is the home of curlews and golden plovers. The Pennine Way tracks north along the backbone of England; only two or three roads chance their way across the wilderness here. All of this adds to the attraction and every now and then there is a sunny day and it is possible to stand on a bank of cloudberry and see for ever.

212

KINDER DOWNFALL

ESSENTIAL SIGHTS

Unmissable attractions

The Dark Peak lies on a bed of millstone grit beneath peat. The surface is a skin of bog moss or cotton grass, the home of grouse, curlew and plover. Only two or three roads cross this wilderness that, surprisingly, still exists less than a dozen miles from the cities of Manchester and Sheffield. The Pennine Way, Britain's first and toughest long-distance footpath, has its southern terminus at Edale, in the shadow of the Peaks highest hill, Kinder Scout. In the nearby Hope Valley, there is so much of interest that Castleton sometimes suffers from a surfeit of tourists, but it is a good base for exploring the area. Castleton is presided over by the impressively sited ruins of Peveril Castle. Deep beneath the castle is Speedwell Cavern, an old lead mine that descends 2,000 feet (600m). For the more adventurous this part of the Peaks has some of Britain's deepest and most challenging caves.

1

1 **Kinder Scout**
Celebrate the climb to the top of Kinder Scout and enjoy the reward of far-reaching views, which take in the silvery Kinder Reservoir.

2 **The Pennine Way**
Edale marks the start of the Pennine Way, for 256 miles (412km) to Kirk Yetholm, just over the border in Scotland.

215

ESSENTIAL SIGHTS

3 Edale

A cyclist tackles the winding Edale road in the Dark Peak. Less arduous routes for cyclists, and walkers, include the Sett Valley Trail which runs from New Mills to Hayfield.

4 Blue John Mine

The mine extends deep into the hillside so, when visiting, remember to wear warm clothes, even on a summer's day, as it is much colder underground than on the surface.

4

WINNATS PASS

CASTLETON

Castles and caves cast a potent spell; Castleton sometimes suffers from a surfeit of tourists, but there is so much of interest along the upper reach of the Hope Valley that it is impossible not to be drawn into the busy little village, at least as a base from which to wander. The curtain of high hills at the head of the valley rises to 1,695 feet (517m) at Mam Tor, less than 2 miles (3.2km) to the northwest of the village. Bands of shale and gritstone give the breast-shaped dome of this 'mother-mountain' a terraced appearance; more importantly, the shale is unstable and the whole hillside is gradually slumping down into the valley, taking the old main road with it. In recent years the fate of the road has drawn as many sightseers as the more conventional tourist attractions in the area.

The tumbled stonework of an Iron Age hill fort rings the top of Mam Tor; hill-forts were a sign of prestige and status among hostile

Visit

OAK APPLE DAY

Oak Apple Day, 29 May, is celebrated in Castleton by a glorious pub crawl, involving a procession led by the 'King' and 'Queen', both in Restoration costume and on horseback; the King is completely covered in a great cone of flowers. A silver band plays the traditional tune *Pudding in a Lantern*, girls dance and everyone welcomes the summer. In Castleton this is known as Garland day; obscure, colourful and intoxicating. The words of a song capture the spirit of the event:

Thou doesno' know, and I dono' know
What they han i' Brada;
An owd cow's head, and a piece o' bread,
And a pudding baked in a lantern

tribes in those faraway times, and this site must have been the power-base of an important chieftain. When the Romans arrived the local community had to learn a new way of life; from 'Celtic cowboys' of the

219

open hills they became hewers and delvers in the dusty darkness of the lead mines. Mining, for galena or lead ore, was a major industry in the Castleton area for the best part of 2,000 years, and it has left its scars. Grassy mounds and tree-lined ditches hide old spoil-heaps and rakes or veins. Many of the spoil-heaps were reworked for other minerals, such as fluorspar and blende, and natural limestone caves were enlarged.

Despite the fact that the Derbyshire mines yield no silver, the area west of Castleton, up the winding road to Winnats Pass, is famous for its Blue John, a deep purple form of fluorspar. The Treak Cliff, Speedwell, Peak Cavern and Blue John Mine 'show caves' are open to the public. Of these, Treak Cliff is an old lead mine, rich in veins of the mineral known as Blue John and is still worked, while the Speedwell Mine is special because the main workings (and the 'Bottomless Pit') can only be

approached by boat, floating along an along an underground 'canal' or flooded tunnel. Peak Cavern, close to Castleton, is set into Castle Hill on the south side of the valley and has a natural entrance – 100 feet (30.5m) across and 50 feet (15.2m) high. All the caves are exciting to explore, even as part of a guided tour.

Castleton owes its name and very existence to Peveril Castle, perched on Castle Hill. Peveril was built by William de Peverel, a favourite of William the Conqueror, in 1076. All mineral rights belonged to the king, who therefore had good reason to set a friend up with an overview of the lucrative lead-mining area. The castle also happened to be in the heart of the Peak Forest, prime hunting country; Normans liked to mix profit with pleasure.

Peveril Castle is managed by English Heritage and is open to the public. The footpath up to it is steep and sometimes slippery, but the views from the curtain wall are exceptionally good.

EDALE

Edale is the name given to the upper reaches of the River Noe as it threads its way through a broad valley of pastures and meadowlands. Five ancient farming communities, the Booths, are scattered along the north slope of the valley, tucked in beneath the desolation of the Kinder plateau but above the wilderness of the river. 'Booths' were barns or cowsheds, refuges for stock and farming families in troubled times; they have grown into hamlets and villages linked by green meadows and twisting lanes.

Grindsbrook Booth lies at the heart of the dale and can be anything but calm on sunny Sundays. Edale is the threshold of the high hills, the access point to Kinder. It marks the start of the Pennine Way, the first long-distance footpath in Britain, and is a magnet for walkers. Sitting outside the Old Nag's Head Inn and watching a constant tide of seriously keen walkers disappearing up the track can be a little daunting; in fact most visitors to Kinder are only there for the day and only go a few miles. For those intending to walk the whole 256 miles (412km) of the Pennine Way, the really testing ground is the high Kinder and Bleaklow plateau: this is a wilderness of sodden peat. But there is good walking on a track before that, from opposite the Old Nag's Head, along a footpath signed Hayfield and westwards along the old packhorse trail.

This route is now well-established as the official start of the Pennine Way, and takes you through Upper Booth and up Jacob's Ladder – a set of zig-zag steps cut into the hillside. Edale Cross marks the meeting of the three wards of the Royal Forest of the Peak, and then it is only a few hundred yards north to Kinder Low and Kinder Downfall, the waterfall that sometimes gets blown uphill in the teeth of the western gales. This is no doubt a stiff walk, but worthwhile for the views to the west are very special.

221

HOLLINS CROSS

Visit

'WHETHER THE WEATHER BE WET'
Edale is not a place to linger in the rain;
60 inches (152cm) a year fall on Kinder,
and the Booths get their share. Nor is
there very much cover. On crisp winter
mornings it can be cold in the valley, as
frost rolls down from the summits, but
this is certainly the time to appreciate the
elemental landscape and the far horizons.

GLOSSOP

Textiles breathed life into Glossop;
there was water power and coal
a-plenty and a workforce who came
from Stockport and Manchester. At
the turn of the 19th century there
were more than 56 mills in the eight
townships of Glossopdale; most
were cotton mills, but there were
also paper mills, ropewalks and
woollen mills. Not many thrived;
those that did modernised with the
times and took to power looms,
which were steam-driven and
needed more water and more coal.

The settlement expanded in the early
19th century under the patronage of
the Duke of Norfolk and at one time
it was named Howard Town (Howard
is the family name of the Duke), to
distinguish it from Old Glossop, the
village uphill to the east.

The name Glossop came from
Glott Hop, 'hop' being a valley and
'glott' a much earlier lord of the
manor. But it was the Howards
who left the greatest mark on the
new community and who were
responsible for most of the town's
important buildings, such as the
Market Hall and the Railway Station.
The heart of Glossop is Norfolk
Square, which still has a prim
elegance and is surrounded by
interesting shops, including a small
heritage centre.

Glossop suffered disastrously
when the cotton industry collapsed
in the 1920s, and it took decades
to recover. Overspill housing from
the 1960s affected the character of
the town too, but there are some
fascinating nooks and crannies.

23
PD&NCFPS
1906

FOOTPATH
TO BIRCH VALE VIA
RIDGE TOP & BRIDLE
R^D TO NEW MILLS &c
OVER THE HILL TOP
ALTITUDE 1085 FEET

EDALE

EDALE

Just beyond the housing estate of Gamesley lies the remains of the Agricolan Roman fort of Melandra Castle, while to the north of the town, near Howard Park, is Mouselow or Castle Hill, with important Bronze Age and Iron Age associations and the site of a motte and bailey built by William de Peverel. Glossop's roads to the east lead to Longdendale and the Snake Pass, while only a few miles to the west is the M67 and Manchester.

HAYFIELD

The picturesque name and rural setting disguise Hayfield's industrial past; the village once hummed and rattled to the sound of cotton and paper mills, calico printing and dye works. It has also resounded to marching feet and cries of protest – in 1830 a mob of 1,000 mill workers gathered to demand a living wage and were dispersed by hussars. Eleven men appeared at Derby Assizes as a result, but the cotton industry was in terminal decline and all the anger was in vain. A century later, on 24 April 1932, Hayfield was the starting point for the 'mass trespass' of ramblers onto Kinder Scout. This protest eventually resulted in 'the right to roam'.

Hayfield is a peaceful little village, catering for tourists of all kinds. It has plenty of little cafés and restaurants with quaint and inventive names. One of the most revealing places to while away a few minutes is by the bridge, next to the courtyard of the Royal Hotel, which looks out over the River Sett, from the war memorial to the jumble of cottages and sloping roofs at the back of Church Street. Near by is St Matthew's Church, built on the foundations of an older church washed away in a flood.

Serious walkers head east out of the village, up and over the green foothills to the russet expanse of the Kinder plateau. Families and other easy-going ramblers head west along the Sett Valley Trail towards New Mills. The car park at the start of this 3-mile (4.8km) trail, separated from the main village by the A624, was once the railway station and the trail follows the course of the single-track line. In its heyday thousands of visitors arrived here from Manchester via the New Mills branch line; Hayfield marked the end of the mill towns and the start of the countryside.

HOLMFIRTH

Before the BBC television series *Last of the Summer Wine* became a national institution, the most famous comic characters to come out of Holmfirth were depicted on postcards published by Bamforths. Saucy seaside cartoons became a serious business for the family firm just after the First World War; they had already pioneered lantern slides and the motion picture industry but were outflanked by Hollywood.

The town of Holmfirth is a gem, built at the confluence of the Holme and the Ribble, where the Norman Earl Warren built a corn mill. For several centuries the lower valley was left to the wild wood and the hilltop towns of Cartworth, Upperthong and Wooldale prospered, combining farming with weaving. There are fine stone farmhouses and cottages on the upper slopes of the valley, often absorbed into the outskirts of the newer town, to tell the tale of prosperity. With the expansion of the cotton mills in the mid-19th century tiers of three-storey terraced cottages sprang up lower and lower into the valley and eventually cotton mills crowded the riverside. The fast-flowing river was harnessed but never tamed; it still floods when the Pennine snows melt too quickly.

Pace yourself in Holmfirth because most of the streets are steep. From Victoria Bridge in the middle of the town it is possible to wander up Penny Lane, round the back of the church where the surrounding hills peep out between chimney pots and sooty walls, and down cobbled lanes worn smooth by

DARK PEAK

Insight

THE PENNINE WAY

When it is spring in the valley and there are daffodils all over Holmfirth it is sobering to look to the west and see the clouds still gathered over Wessenden and Saddleworth Moors, and the snow lying on the summit of Black Hill. It looks a frightening prospect, but thousands of walkers tackle it each year as part of the Pennine Way National Trail. The Pennine Way has existed for more than 40 years, and in that time places like Featherbed Moss and Wessenden Head have gained notoriety, quite deserved, for their evil bogs. These days most of the worst bits are stone-flagged to create causey paths like the old packhorse trails. Even so, the Pennine Way is a challenge, and the pubs and guesthouses of Holmfirth are a welcome diversion.

a million clogs. Along the way you should arrive at Sid's Café, or The Wrinkled Stocking Café, next door to Nora Batty's on the river.

HOPE

The Hope Valley is the main access route from the Derwent Valley through to Castleton, Edale and the Dark Peak, so the road is often busy. The little village of Hope lies at the confluence of the Noe and the Peakshole Water, which emerges as if from the bowels of the earth 2 miles (3.2km) away at Castleton. Hope railway station lies half a mile (800m) out of the village, across the Noe to the east, and is a perfect starting point for a walk up Win Hill, one of the best bracing viewpoints in the whole Peak. Lose Hill, the dark twin of Win Hill and another fine viewpoint, lies due west on the opposite side of the Noe.

Hope Church is in the heart of the village and is a typically solid, squat-spired affair, which dates back to the 14th century. Inside there are two stone coffin lids bearing hunting horns, the motif of royal forest huntsmen. Outside, by the porch, is the shaft of a Saxon cross with weathered carvings on its face.

230

HOLMFIRTH

HOPE VALLEY

Stone scrollwork on preaching crosses represents the height of Dark Age culture and the Peak District has some fine examples.

South of Hope stands the Blue Circle cement works, undeniably a blot on the skyline and difficult to reconcile with a National Park except as a source of local employment (but perhaps tourists of the future will come specially to see it, just as today's visitors explore old lead workings and derelict mills). Other landscape features are dwarfed in the presence of this monolith, but it marks the dividing line between the gritstone and limestone; the fields to the south are bright green and enclosed in an intricate mesh of grey drystone walls.

The village of Bradwell lies only a couple of miles from Hope but it is completely different in character, full of steep twisty lanes and lead-miners' cottages. A ridge called the Grey Ditch climbs the slope to Rebellion Knoll and may be a trace of the boundary between the Dark Age kingdoms of Mercia and Northumbria. Near by, accessible by a riverside path from Hope, lies the site of a Roman fort. The stonework was plundered long ago to build local farmhouses and Hope church.

LANGSETT

The northeast corner of the Peaks is probably the least visited sweep of country for 50 miles (80.5km) around; driving south from Holmfirth or west from Penistone takes you across open moors and plateaux with the whole of Yorkshire spread out below in a cerulean haze. There are very few villages to catch your immediate attention, but the upper valleys of the Don and the Porter, which rise on the same watershed as the Derwent on Howden Moor, are full of interest. The Porter has been dammed in several places above Stocksbridge and there are good access points to the reservoirs and riverside and high up onto the moors. Langsett provides the best starting point for an exploration of the Porter and its string of pearls. Before Sheffield Corporation bought up the valley for water catchment this area was farmland, with some of the finest medieval cruck-framed farmhouses and barns in the country. Many of the buildings survive today, some still as dwellings but few as working farms.

Langsett Barn bears a datestone of 1621 and is now the village hall but it is open during the season as a National Park Information Centre, and is worth a visit both for information and displays about the park and to see the solid functional beauty of the barn's ancient post and truss construction.

Heading out from the car park it is possible to explore the woodlands and shoreline of Langsett Reservoir or walk along the dam wall, past the crenellated valve tower (a miniature of a tower at Lancaster Castle), to the old stone-built hamlet of Upper Midhope. Above Langsett Reservoir, the Brook House Bridge gives access to the ancient trackway of the Cut

Gate, an old drovers' road which started at Derwent and leads all the way to Penistone. The track climbs south over Midhope Moor, which is uncompromising high ground inhabited mostly by mountain hares and short-eared owls, littered with ancient flints and overlooked by the burial mound of Pike Lowe.

LONGDENDALE

Above Glossop a cleft in the most desolate wilderness of Peak moorland runs north by northeast from the little town of Tintwistle to the Derbyshire-Yorkshire border, shielding the A628 as it climbs to Gallows Moss. Down the cleft runs the River Etherow, a tributary of the Mersey. Over a century ago the valley was dammed to create five reservoirs, and this has so altered the character of the place that it sometimes looks like an oasis in a desert; green woodland and pasture encircle pools of silver, criss-crossed by an array of colourful sailing dinghies and windsurfers.

Longdendale is a favourite place for day trips out of Manchester, and the cultural roots of Tintwistle are entwined with the old Lancashire cotton mills. The waters of the Etherow were harnessed to power the mills and were dammed to provide water for the city. A wealth of railway lines were laid to link the great industrial cities of Manchester and Sheffield, following the valley up to Woodhead and the Prough, a 3-mile (4.8km) tunnel below the moors. But now all that is in the distant past; the weavers' cottages of Tintwistle are now picturesque and the course of the railway is a footpath. Nevertheless, the dale still serves the city in its own way and remains part of its heritage.

The graveyard of lonely Woodhead Chapel, set on a shoulder above the banks of the upper reservoir, contains the last resting place of navvies and their families who died of cholera while the second railway tunnel was being built in 1849. Crowden, above Torside Reservoir, is a famous youth hostel on the route of the Pennine Way and is a welcome sight to walkers after the rigours of Bleaklow to the south or Black Hill to the north. Apart from a few isolated farms and an Information Centre there are no other settlements in the valley; despite fine scenery Longdendale often suffers from a wild climate, in the shadow of the moors.

SADDLEWORTH

The gorge of the river Tame forms the boundary of the National Park in the northwest. Slicing between Saddleworth Moor and the West Pennines, this defile hosts a string of picturesque gritstone villages that breathe Yorkshire charm and character into an area with a history stretching back to the Romans (the site of a fortlet stands beside the remote reservoirs at Castleshaw). Saddleworth itself is a nebulous area; there's no village of that name here – the great sweep of moors arcing west from Holmfirth, and the villages on it, take that collective name. This area was part of Yorkshire's West Riding until 1974 and is decidedly proud of this fact. The largest village is Uppermill, strung alongside the Huddersfield Narrow Canal and crammed with craft and antique shops, restaurants and inns; the Saddleworth Museum has a succinct overview of the area. Just to the north, locks rise to Britain's longest canal tunnel at Standedge, for over 3 miles (4.8km).

The most charismatic village is Dobcross, huddled around a tiny cobbled square stapled to the end of Harrop Edge, from which narrow lanes and ginnels lined with three-storey weaver's cottages plummet to old mills in the valley bottom. Film buffs may recognise the square from the 1979 film *Yanks*. Further up the Tame, Delph retains perhaps the most 'industrial' feel of all the villages, its mills gradually morphing into trendy apartments below bluffs and crags smothered by bilberry and heather.

Visit

WHAT IS A NATIONAL PARK?

Britain's National Parks are not national property. Most of the land is still privately owned, but the area is administered by a National Park Authority. It is their task to strike an appropriate – and often fragile – balance between the conservation of the park's landscape, architecture and wildlife, while still ensuring that the local people and landowners can make a living and that the millions of visitors and walkers have access to use and appreciate the park's landscape. The National Park Authority in the Peak District operates a number of Information Centres, such as the one at Langsett, which provides a wide range of information, publications and organises walks and talks in and about the area.

Linking these and the other villages of Saddleworth is the remarkable Longwood Thump Rushcart Festival. Held over the second weekend after the 12 August, this celebration centres on a cart,

237

DARK PEAK

Visit

THE SNAKE PASS INN
The Snake Inn was built in 1821 as Lady Clough House, when the original medieval track was transformed into a turnpike road. If any visitor should need a reminder about how remote this hostelry is, there is a milestone outside the inn that records the 21 miles to Manchester and 17 miles to Sheffield. The low stone-built inn is an ideal place to stop for refreshment. Food is served most days of the week and is a range of accommodation is available.

pulled by teams of men, that is decorated by a high pyramid of rushes, atop which a hapless soul must sit in a chair while touring the churches and inns of the area. The phrase 'Going on the Wagon' is said to originate here.

A visit to the Church Inn, high above Uppermill, where the festival is based, will reveal much. In the graveyard next door is a fascinating memorial to victims of a double

murder – the 'Bill o' Jacks murders', unsolved since 1832. Myriad footpaths string southwards to some fine, challenging walks around and above Dovestone Reservoir, set in a landscape of cloughs, moors, edges and wind-sculpted pinnacles.

THE SNAKE PASS
Weather warnings on television and radio have made The Snake Pass famous; when the sun is shining across the rest of the Pennines, The Snake Pass, the A57 between Sheffield and Manchester, may be closed because of severe blizzards.

The road from Ladybower and the Woodlands Valley strikes northwest, sheltered on a shoulder of the River Ashop, but after Lady Clough it has nowhere to hide and crosses a windswept peat desert at 1,680 feet (512m). Bleaklow lies to the north, Kinder Scout to the south. In places the peat has been stripped away to reveal a surface of shattered stones, which is how the glaciers left the place after the Ice Age. There are

FAIRBROOK, NEAR KINDER SCOUT

no trees, no barns or walls. Not a good place to be stuck in a car.

Of course, the remote wildness of The Snake is irresistible and in fine weather, with the sun shining on the heather, it can be magical. The upper Woodlands Valley is pretty, dotted with old farms and birch-lined cloughs. Most of the Peak District has been designated as an Environmentally Sensitive Area, which means that farmers get special payments for agreeing to manage the land with conservation as a priority. In the case of the high moors, the most important thing is the stocking rate – fewer sheep are now overwintered on the heather, and this should benefit the flora and fauna.

A tributary of the Ashop runs north to Alport Dale and Alport Castle, which is not a castle at all, but an outcrop of rock; this is accessible by a bridleway and makes a good walk. The barn of Alport Castle Farm is used on the first Sunday in July each year for a Lovefeast service. These 'love feasts' originated during the 18th-century religious revival that was spearheaded by the Wesley brothers. They converted multitudes of workers, from mines and mills, farms and factories, to a pattern of religious life which inspired them to build a number of 'wayside Bethels' in remote places. Along with field preaching, their ministers organised camp meetings and covenant services, incorporating 'love feasts', which were based on the meetings of the early Church.

Back along the Snake Road there are two or three last farms and cottages before you reach the lonely Snake Pass Inn. At the top of Lady Clough, on the highest and most featureless ground, The Snake is crossed by the Pennine Way, close to the paved trackway of ancient Doctor's Gate.

Travellers have been venturing across these atmospheric moors for thousands of years, often with a shiver of apprehension.

DARK PEAK

TOURIST INFORMATION CENTRES
Holmfirth
49–51 Huddersfield Road.
Tel: 01484 222444
Saddleworth
High Street, Uppermill, Oldham.
Tel: 01457 870336

NATIONAL PARK CENTRES
Visit all under
www.peakdistrict.gov.uk
Castleton
Cross Street (main car park).
Tel: 01433 620679
Edale
Fieldhead (right of road from
Edale Station to village).
Tel: 01433 670207
Fairholmes (Derwent Valley)
Tel: 01433 650953

PLACES OF INTEREST
Blue John Cavern
1m (1.6km) west of Castleton
via Winnats Pass.
Tel: 01433 620638;
www.bluejohn-cavern.co.uk

**Last of the Summer
Wine Exhibition**
Huddersfield Road, Holmfirth.
Tel: 01484 681408
Peak Cavern
Castleton, village centre.
Tel: 01433 620285;
www.devilsarse.com
Peveril Castle
Castleton.
Tel: 01433 620613;
www.english-heritage.org.uk
**Saddleworth Llama Trekking
& Animal Farm**
High Oxhey Farm, Denshaw.
Tel: 01457 810186;
www.saddleworthllamatrekking.com
Walk with llamas in the moors and
valleys of Saddleworth.
Saddleworth Museum
High Street, Uppermill.
Tel: 01457 874093;
www.saddleworthmuseum.co.uk
Speedwell Cavern
0.5 miles (800m) west of Castleton
at Winnats Pass.
Tel: 01433 620512;
www.speedwellcavern.co.uk

Treak Cliff Cavern
0.75 miles (1.2km) west of Castleton.
Tel: 01433 620571;
www.bluejohnstone.com

SHOPPING
Castleton
Farmers' Market, first Sun each month.
Glossop
Indoor market, Thu; indoor and
outdoor market, Fri and Sat.
Holmfirth
Craft market, Sat and Bank Hols.
Farmers' Market, 3rd Sun each month.
General market, Thu.

LOCAL SPECIALITIES
Blue John Jewellery
Speedwell Caverns Ltd,
Winnats Pass, Castleton.
Tel: 01433 620512
Also available from other local outlets.
Craft workshops
Glossop Craft Centre,
No 1 Smithy Fold, off
High Street East, Glossop.
Tel: 01457 863559;
www.glossopmaycrafts.co.uk

SPORTS & ACTIVITIES
ANGLING
Arnfield Reservoir
Tintwistle.
Tel: 01457 856269;
www.arnfield-fly-fishery.com
BOAT TRIPS
Saddleworth
Pennine Moonraker Canal Cruises.
Tel: 0161 652 6331;
www.saddleworth-canal-cruises.co.uk
CAVING
Edale
YHA Activity Centre,
Rowland Cote, Nether Booth.
Tel: 01433 670302;
www.yha.org.uk
Hathersage
Rock Lea Activity Centre,
Station Road.
Tel: 01433 650345;
www.iain.co.uk
COUNTRY PARK
Etherow Country Park
George Street,
Compstall,
Stockport.
Tel: 0161 4276937

CYCLING
Longdendale Trail
A 6-mile (9.7km) multi-user trail from
Hadfield to Woodhead Tunnels.
The Sett Valley Trail
This trail runs for 2.5 miles (4km) from
New Mills to Hayfield.
CYCLE HIRE
Glossop
Peak Tours
Tel: 01457 851462;
www.peak-tours.com
Hayfield
Old Railway Station.
Tel: 01663 746222;
www.peakdistrict.org
GUIDED WALKS
National Park Walks with a Ranger
Contact Peak District National Park.
Tel: 01629 816200;
www.peakdistrict.org.uk
New Mills
Peak Outdoor Training, Marsh Road,
New Mills, Derbyshire.
Tel: 01663 743278
www.peakoutdoortraining.co.uk
Guided walks, also rock climbing,
canoeing and other adventure sports.

Peak District
Annual Peak District Walking Festival.
Large programme of guided walks
held in late Apr/early May.
Tel: 0870 444 7275;
www.visitpeakdistrict.com/walk
HANG- AND PARA-GLIDING
Peak Airsports
Joan Lane, Bamford.
Tel: 07703 062721;
www.peakairsports.com
HORSE-RIDING
Edale
Lady Booth Riding Centre.
Tel: 01433 670205
**LONG-DISTANCE FOOTPATHS
AND TRAILS**
The Limestone Way
A 46-mile (74km) route south
from Castleton to Rocester
(Staffordshire).
The Pennine Bridleway
Aimed at horse-riders and
cyclists, but also useful to walkers.
A lengthy 350 miles (563km) from
Cromford via the Dark Peak to
Byrness (Northumberland).

The Pennine Way
Runs for 256 miles (412km) from Edale to Kirk Yetholm just in Scotland.
The Sett Valley Trail
This trail runs for 2.5 miles (4km), from New Mills to Hayfield.
ROCK-CLIMBING
Edale
Edale YHA Activity Centre, Rowland Cote, Nether Booth.
Tel: 0870 770 5808
Hathersage
Rock Lea Activity Centre, Peak Activities Ltd, Station Road.
Tel: 01433 650345;
www.iain.co.uk
WATERSPORTS
Hathersage
Rock Lea Activity Centre, Peak Activities Ltd, Station Road. Also helicopter rides.
Tel: 01433 650345;
www.iain.co.uk

ANNUAL EVENTS & CUSTOMS
Visit www.visitpeakdistrict.com
Alport Castle
Alport Love Feast in Alport Barn. Access via Heyridge Farm on A57, early Jul.
Castleton
Garland Ceremony, 29 May.
Glossop
Jazz Festival, mid-Jun.
Carnival and Country Fair, early Jul.
Victorian weekend, early Sep.
Well dressing and Padfield Plum Fair, Sep.
Hayfield
Well dressing, mid-Jul.
Sheepdog Trials, Sep.
Holmfirth
Folk Festival, early May.
Hope
Well dressing, late Jun–early Jul.
Sheepdog Trials and Agricultural Show, late Aug.
Saddleworth
Brass band contest, Whit Friday.
Folk Festival, late Jul.
Longwood Thump Rushcart Festival, late Aug.

TEA ROOMS

Jamaica Blue
56 High Street, Uppermill,
Saddleworth OL3 6HA
Tel: 01457 870555
www.jamaicablue.co.uk
A stylish café-bar beside the River
Tame and close to a museum, canal
and parks. The new riverside patio
is a peaceful retreat at which to chow
down with teas and coffees, sweet
treats, ciabattas, snacks or even
filling meals.

Rose Cottage Café
Cross Street, Castleton,
Derbyshire S33 8WH
Tel: 01433 620472
www.rosecottagecastleton.co.uk
Climbing plants decorate the outside
of this traditional English teashop. At
the rear is a secluded patio. There's
an excellent choice of freshly prepared
food, including cream teas, grand
sandwiches, home-baked cakes,
steaming bowls of soup and
great coffee.

The Wrinkled Stocking Tea Room
Huddersfield Road, Holmfirth,
West Yorkshire HD9 2JS
Tel: 01484 681408
www.wrinkledstocking.co.uk
Cool pastel walls and crisp tablecloths
– just what Nora Batty would expect!
Located at those famous steps at
Compo's house (now an exhibition),
indulge in home-baked speciality
pastries and cakes and good Yorkshire
tea. Sid's Café (Tel: 01484 689610) is
a short stroll away, near the church.

Woodbine Café
Castleton Road, Hope,
Derbyshire S33 6AA
Tel: 01433 621407
www.woodbine-hope.co.uk
A welcoming, homely stone terraced
cottage, with a sheltered tea garden,
not far from Hope's distinctive
church. Within, it is cosy and tranquil,
appetising aromas of home-baking
mingling with quiet conversation or the
crackle of logs on a winter fire. They
also offer B&B.

DRYSTONE WALL

MAM TOR

The Church Inn
Pob Green, Uppermill
(Saddleworth) OL3 6LW
Tel: 01457 820902
Splendid food is twinned with tasty beers brewed in the cellar. Memorabilia from the Rushcart Festival held each August is scattered about. Views from this most welcoming gritstone pub, high above the Tame Valley are stunning. As you might guess from its name, it is situated next to the church.

Cheshire Cheese Inn
Edale Road, Hope,
Derbyshire S33 6ZF
Tel: 01433 620381
A compact, cheerful local with a warm welcome guaranteed. The landlord is keen on stocking beers from some of the Peak District's many microbreweries and offers an ever-changing menu using local produce whenever possible.

Pack Horse Inn
Mellor Road, New Mills,
Derbyshire SK22 4QQ
Tel: 01663 742365
www.packhorseinn.co.uk
High above New Mills, the inn has an enviable position with views to the great moorland plateau of Kinder. It's a lovely stone-built place with a growing reputation for good wholesome food and an eclectic choice of real ales.

The Royal Hotel
Market Street, Hayfield,
Derbyshire SK22 2EP
Tel: 01663 741721
www.theroyalhayfield.co.uk
At the hub of the village, this grandiose inn has a patio where you can enjoy the local beers and take in the views of Kinder Scout. Inside, find a peaceful corner and tuck in to filling pub grub – there's usually a good fish menu.

USEFUL INFORMATION

**PEAK DISTRICT NATIONAL PARK
INFORMATION POINT**
**Peak District National Park
Headquarters**
Head Office, Aldern House, Baslow
Road, Bakewell, Derbyshire DE45 1AE
Tel: 01629 816200;
www.peakdistrict.gov.uk

OTHER INFORMATION
Angling
Numerous opportunities for fishing on
farms, lakes and rivers. Permits and
licences are available from local tackle
shops and TICs.
Cheshire Wildlife Trust
Bickley Hall Farm, Bickley
Malpas, Cheshire SY14 8EF
Tel: 01948 820728;
www.cheshirewildlifetrust.co.uk

Derbyshire Wildlife Trust
East Mill, Bridge Foot,
Belper DE56 1HX.
Tel: 01773 881188;
www.derbyshirewildlifetrust.org.uk
English Heritage
Canada House, 3 Chepstow Street,
Manchester.
Tel: 0161 242 1400;
www.english-heritage.org.uk
Environment Agency
PO Box 544, Rotherham,
South Yorkshire S60 1BY
Tel: 08708 506506
The National Trust
East Midlands Regional Office,
Clumber Park Stableyard, Worksop,
Nottinghamshire S80 3AZ
Tel: 01909 4863411;
www.nationaltrust.org.uk
Natural England
'Endcliffe', Deepdale Business Park,
Ashford Road, Bakewell DE45 1GT
Tel: 0300 060 2228

Parking
Most urban and many rural car parks in Derbyshire and the Peak District area are pay-and-display. Period visitors' parking tickets are available to personal callers from National Park Visitor Centres and cycle hire centres, or apply in writing to the Peak District National Park Head Office at Bakewell, Derbyshire.

Places of Interest
There will be an admission charge unless otherwise stated. We give details of just some of the facilities within the area covered by this guide. Further information can be obtained from local TICs or the web.

Public Transport
'Derbyshire Wayfarer' allows one day's unlimited travel on all local buses and trains. Details from Derbyshire County Council, Public Transport Dept.
Tel: 01629 536738
Bus services in Derbyshire
Tel: 0871 200 2233;
www.derbysbus.info
GMPTE Tel: 0161 244 1000;
SYPTE Tel: 01709 515151
Rail information.
Tel: 08457 484950
Staffordshire Wildlife Trust
The Wolseley Centre, Wolseley Bridge, Stafford ST17 0WT
Tel: 01889 880100;
www.staffordshirewildlife.org.uk
Weather
Tel: 0906 850 0412;
www.weathercall.co.uk

INDEX

A

Alport Castle 241
Arbor Low 146-7, **148**
Arkwright, Richard 165, 180, 184, 185
Ashbourne 17, 28, 31, 32, **33-4**
Ashbourne-Buxton Railway 40
Ashford in the Water 112-13, 115, 116, **117-21**
Axe Edge 44, 95

B

Bakewell 110, 112, 115, 120, **121-2**
Bakewell Pudding 115, 120, **121**
Baslow **164**
Beeley 173, 174
Belper 28
Beresford, Thomas 52
Beresford Dale 36, 40
Bertram, St 43
bilberries **173**
Black Hill 212, 230, 236
Black Rock 52
Bleaklow 212, 221, 236, 238

Blue John Mine 216, 217, 220
Boil Holes 43
Bonsall Brook 182-3, 185
Boswell, James 43
Bradford Dale 148
Bradwell 233
Brassington 35
Brindley, James 85, **86**, 135
Bronze Age 45, 142, 164, 197, 228
Brown, 'Capability' 168
Burne-Jones, Edward 149, 189
Buxton 64, 67, **68-77**

C

Caldon Canal 85
Calver 163, **165**
Carsington Water **34-6**
Castle Hill 122, 149, 220, 228
Castleton 23, 218, **219-20**, 230
Cat and Fiddle Moor 64, 81
Chapel-en-le-Frith 64, 76, **77-8**
Charlie, Bonnie Prince 33
Chatsworth 86, 160, 163, 164, **168-74**
Chesterfield 125, 160, **174-7**
Churchtown 185-9

Churnet, River 85, 86
Civil War **77**
Combs Moss 78, 136
Combs Reservoir 78
Cotton, Charles 40
Cratcliffe Rocks 145, 149
Cressbrook Dale 135, 144, **145**
Crich **177-80**
Cromford **180-5**
Cromford and High Peak Railway 36, 184
Cromford Canal 53, 184
Cromford Moor 52
Curbar 6, 158, 163, **165**, 166-7, 207
Cut Gate 234

D

Dane, River 64, 96
Danebridge 96
Dark Peak 10, 15, **210-51**
Darley Dale **185-9**
deer **168**
Defoe, Daniel 10, 142
Delph 237
Derbyshire Bridge 81
Derbyshire Dales 127, 145
Derwent Dams **189-92**
Derwent Reservoir 189, 190
Derwent Valley **158-209**, 230

252

INDEX

254

ACKNOWLEDGEMENTS

256